THE SURVIVAL GROUP

STANDARD OPERATING PROCEDURE
BLUEPRINT

By Alton Gabriel

INTRODUCTION

Sustained survival isn't a singleton operation. There are plenty of resources that outline how to survive in the wilderness or to bug out to a set location. True survival will rely on the assistance of others and this book will help you establish your survival group.

What the book is: a guide to establishing your survival group.

What this book is not: an all-encompassing guide on tactics or any other sections included in the book.

Think of this as your 90 percent solution. Why would it not be a 100 percent solution? One standard set of procedures is not appropriate for the wide variety of human and physical terrain. Additionally, group members bring a diversity of skills and backgrounds that will affect your group's product. Finally, your SOP needs to be yours. The act of everyone contributing creates ownership and buy-in to how the group operates.

My background in military operations and experience during hurricanes, including Katrina, aided in the creation of this book. I am confident that this book provides the architecture to create the SOP that meets your group's unique solutions.

SOP's are always evolving. As such, there will be future updates to this book that will add or clarify content. An 80% plan today is better than a 100% plan that never happens. Consider this as it pertains to your group. Get started on your group's way forward and continually improve.

Table of Contents

DIGITAL SECURITY

Security is defined as procedures implemented individually and collectively for protection against illicit activity. Security is the first topic discussed because security should come first in all that we do.

Security can be taught but more so is a set of habits. These habits should be implemented now. Civil unrest is an often a slow process in which the security situation degrades over time. We must be prepared to protect ourselves in today's world and look ahead to plan how to protect ourselves during a shift of society or total collapse. Security can be broken down in several types. The first area of security we will discuss is digital.

YOUR PERSONAL ONLINE SECURITY

Out increasing reliance on the internet for everything from how we shop, to how we bank, and how we do business is a major threat. These security breaches – from Hope Depot, Sony, LinkedIn, Yahoo!, and the Ashley Madison dating site, has taught us that no one is immune.

Most every one of us uses the Internet, be it through a computer, tablet or phone. This means that over the years, you have managed to build a pretty strong reputation online: opening up email accounts, joining social media, commenting on forums, creating blog posts, online banking, purchasing online and use of online payment systems, Internet dating you name it.

The increasing reliance on the Internet also means bad actors – data scrapers, spammers, identity thieves, job search scams and other nefarious online characters – can now boast of more 'attack points" from which they can steal your personal information. After all, personal information is *personal* for a reason.

Fortunately, there are a couple of key measures we can take to ensure we stay safe and anonymous online. The ones we will be focusing on include: Better password management, using encrypted network channels, safeguarding your personal information on social media platforms, Use of TOR/Onion routers

PASSWORD STRENGTH AND MANAGEMENT

The big issue with passwords is that most of us choose policies of efficiency at the expense of security. Password management is both a choice and a habit. The best practices can only minimize your level of risk. Having a strong password plan is one of the biggest favors you can do yourself in a bid to stay safe online. Fortunately, it is not a hard thing to do if you follow a few simple guidelines.

Create Strong Passwords: Many people assume that with password strength, the lengthier the better. While length is arguably the biggest factor in a strong password equation, length alone is not enough. You have to consider entropy (how random a password is). The more random a password is, the less predictable it is. By "random" we mean the use of additional character sets (think symbols, numbers, unicode).

Length + entropy = stronger password

PASSPHRASES

A password needs to be one you can remember. This conflict to create longer, easy-to-remember passwords has led to a lot of people creating long but common password. These long but easy passwords are easy to guess. There is a workaround, passphrases. Passphrases are passwords based off phrases that are easily memorable.

For example, Iliveinsandiegocalifornia, which you can combine with numbers and symbols to become: Iliv5inS@ndi5goC@liforni@

The previous is a strong password. Assuming, of course, not honest about where you live. Lies are allowed when it comes to passwords.

One way to test the strength of your passwords is to check them on PassFault.com, a brainchild of a computer security expert.

DO NOT REUSE PASSWORDS

Reusing the same or an almost similar password across multiple sites is not recommended. It may be convenient for you, true, but this will only simplify things for attackers.

Other sources have suggested that passwords can be reused by choosing the same base and then incorporating the website name in one form or another. What this does is make it easy to guess all your other passwords, the last thing you want. Any form of password reuse is not advisable because should one account be compromised, it is only a matter of time before the other accounts suffer a similar fate.

USE A PASSWORD MANAGER

The good thing about password managers is that all you need to do is create a very strong master password that you can be using to log in to the application. As for the individual passwords for each account you have, the password manager will generate (and fill) them for you, as well as warn you about unsafe sites.

Putting all your eggs in one basket means the lock needs to be virtually unbreakable. Many people rely on pen and paper but the downside to this is that it is susceptible to loss and theft. A better option to store your master password would be to generate a password card. This is basically a card filled with a mishmash of random characters, and you alone know where your password starts and ends.

SECURE/ENCRYPTED CHANNELS

A secure/encrypted channel is basically the use of the SSL/TLS connection to secure your web communications through HTTPS, a type of online connection based on a security certificate. This certificate guarantees that the website you are using is both credible, and that any sensitive data keyed in will get to its intended destination safely.

In the process, your identity is kept safe from any eavesdroppers that may include anyone from your ISP, to the government or probably mobile operators, as well as man-in-the-middle attacks.

If you want to know if you are on a secure channel, the letters "https" (note the "s") should appear at the beginning of the website's URL. You can also look for a little symbol that resembles a locked padlock on the address bar.

Today, it has become very easy for anyone to pry on your Internet activities, especially when you are accessing the web through a public connection. If you can, abstain from typing in passwords when using public connections, particularly for high-value sites such as e-commerce and banking sites.

Consider subscribing to a VPN service. A virtual private network is an extension of a private network across a public network like the Internet. It allows you to send and receive data as if you were directly using a private network. You can find plenty of VPN services online.

If you want to stay completely anonymous when making online payments, avoid credit cards and online payment systems such as PayPal. A cryptocurrency such as bitcoin or any of its competitors will keep you off the grid.

SAFEGUARDING INFORMATION ON SOCIAL MEDIA

We all love spending time on social networks, both for personal and professional reasons. As with all things Internet though, they too are inherently dangerous. Cyber criminals can and are using them for more than just unearthing your private information: there is the threat of delivering spam or malware; stalking and bulling.

Yet not many people go to out of their way to protect themselves.

The first thing you need to come to terms with regard to social media is that nothing you put out there is private. And with sites like Facebook updating their privacy policy regularly, you never know who is aware of something you thought was never in public view.

Some of these platforms have made it fairly straightforward to customize your privacy settings.

SOME MEASURES YOU CAN TAKE TO SAFEGUARD YOUR SOCIAL MEDIA INFORMATION INCLUDE THE FOLLOWING:

Make use of the privacy features available. Limit the information you share online to only people you know to prevent strangers from accessing that information. You never know who could be looking.

Use a strong password unique for every platform. A password manager could come in handy in this regard. You can beef it up the more by incorporating two-factor authentication for those social networks that offer this option.

Use social network protection. For starters, you need to have a strong, up-to-date antivirus in place. The best programs out there (e.g. Kaspersky Total Security/Bitdefender Total Security) have special filters that sniff out social network-targeted attacks.

Watch out for scams. There is no shortage of scams doing the rounds on social media, from simple questionnaires looking to know something about your tastes, to the more serious ones out to trick you into giving away your password or credit card number by downloading malware.

Rethink how you share using GPS-enabled devices. Some of us have made it a habit of living like an open book by updating the world on every sweet little nothing we are up to. If you can, avoid sharing photos of your current whereabouts, and if you can't, then choose to share after the fact.

USE TOR/ONION ROUTERS

There are many ways of achieving anonymity online, but one of the most common methods to use is through a software known as Tor, commonly referred to as the "onion router".

The open-source program is free and contains multiple applications such as a network, a browser, a webmail service, an IM program, large file transfer service and more – all tools designed to keep you and your connection incognito on the web. Call it the total package.

The underlying idea behind Tor is to have this spiraling, hard-to-follow electronic route that throws off anyone who may be thinking of tailing you, and then erasing your digital footprints periodically. It's a dream.

It is necessary to point out that using Tor is slow, but if you are looking to opt out of getting tracked on the web, then this is your best bet. Using Tor is not illegal, with some of its most popular users including the U.S. Navy, governments, NGOs and journalists looking to communicate safely with dissidents and whistleblowers.

LAST WORD

None of these anonymity methods is foolproof, but the more of them you add to your online privacy arsenal, the safer it will be for you and the harder for anyone to identify you. Most times, achieving online privacy means experiencing inconveniences in your online life, but if you are serious about it, there is no other easy way out. Those who hack and monitor our activities live in the hope that most web users follow the easy way out and take little to no measures of protecting their online identities. This continues to be the case, as the multiple data breaches of the last six or so years have proven. Do your part and make sure not to end up being a statistic.

PERSONAL SECURITY

PERSONAL SECURITY: Personal Security is a set of procedures implemented individually to protect oneself. Some of these habits are listed below and in the individual contingency plans outlined later.

- Always be aware of your surroundings; develop your situational awareness

- Understand your environment; avoid areas of high crime and identify situations outside the norm.

- Blend in and don't be a target; wear clothes and jewelry acceptable for the environment.

- Always assume you are being watched.

- Protect any personal identifying information; keep your online signature low.

- Assess everyone you cross; develop your ability to read nonverbal communications. Facial expressions and body language can show intent.

- Always know your exits and have an idea where safe havens can be located.

- Work and move in groups of two or more

OPERATIONAL SECURITY: The US Department of Defense defines Operations Security, or OPSEC, as the process by which we protect unclassified information that can be used against us. We will define OPSEC as the process which we protect information that can compromise our survival activities. You and your preparations could become a target during a disaster or a shift in society. As the World War II saying goes, "loose lips sink ships." People talk, and you never know who will receive this information or their intent.

Keep the specifics or your prepping activities off of the internet. Online blogs, forums, and videos are almost irreplaceable resource to learn and share information regarding preparedness and survival. Its encouraged to use these tools for learning and the sharing of information. When online, you will leave a trail of information that can be easily connected unless you follow these guidelines.

- Do not use your name or other identifying information for user names or email addresses.

- Consider using a different user names and email addresses for different forums.

- Don't use email addresses that are also linked to credit cards. When sites are hacked, your home address will be linked to your online profiles.

- Use strong passwords

- Don't post photos that have faces or other identifying information in the background.

- Make sure any photos posted have Meta Data deleted. Meta data digitally records camera settings and even GPS location on certain cameras and enabled smart photo.

Threat Profiling: Threat or Threat profiling is a method of proactively identifying threats based on human behavior. The key word is proactively. In Left of Bang, Patrick Van Horne and Jason A. Riley discuss this method and explains how to identify threat by using six domains; Kinesics, Biometric Cues, Proxemics, Geographics, Iconography, and Atmospherics (Van Horne, Riley 67).

Kinesics: This is a big word that simply means the study of body language. Humans have inherited the ability to read signals gleaned from body language. The combined facial movements for happiness, sadness, contempt, anger, and surprise are easily identified in controlled settings. In a fast-paced environment, these same movements, displayed as micro expressions, may not be as easy to identify. Body posture is easier to identify and harder to mask. When the body is preparing to fight, posture is adjusted to look larger and more dominant. Is the individual watching and assessing you or other individuals in the area? Are the individual's feet facing towards you or another individual in the area? This could signal focus. Anticipation can express itself with hand or foot twitches.

Biometric Cues: Biometric cues are uncontrollable reactions to stress. An individual with a reddening of the face or neck could be angry or ready to react. Dilated pupils may be associated with anxiety or fear. When a person is extremely focused, blinking rates are slowed. Perspiration or dry mouth can also indicate nervousness. (Van Horne, Riley 70).

Proxemics: The study of space and movement between individuals is Proxemics. The personal zone is space reserved for friends and acquaintances. This area varies from culture to culture. In western society, this space is within arm's reach. Sometimes in society this zone is breached. The examples would be an elevator or on crowded public transportation (Van Horne, Riley 106). Proximity at a checkout line combined with other cues from other domains could indicate intent. Additionally, the way a person positions oneself around oneself could be an indicator. Is the person positioned between you and an escape route? Movement, specifically the way a person moves can also show intent. An individual following and matching speed while walking could indicate you are being followed. A person approaching you at gas pump should alert you as it is usually outside social norms.

Geographics: This is commonly referred to as knowing your operational environment. What are the local demographics and crime? Using online tools can give you a history of crime in an area and predict what crimes will happen. Some of these websites include Spotcrime.com, the National Public Sex Defender Public Website, and Crimereports.com. Understanding your operational environment can also help you identify who should or should not be in the area, this leads into Iconography (Van Horne, Riley 117).

Iconography: This is the manner in which individuals express what they believe in. Individuals do this by the clothing they wear, their hairstyles, colors they choose, tattoos, and jewelry. People who dress in a way to present you themselves as outside social norms are not necessarily a threat; it should be considered with cues from other domains. Emblems on shirts and vehicles, flags on houses, or graffiti on buildings all provide insight into feelings in the area (Van Horne, Riley 130).

Atmospherics: Using all the previous domains, you can gain insight regarding on the attitude of an area. Is it hostile? Are there individuals exhibiting cues that don't fit in? "Shifts" in atmospherics from positive to negative are often an indicator of imminent threat.

REACT TO HOME INVASION:

A home invasion is a burglary in which the house is occupied. According to FBI statistics, home invasions often involve assaults, rape, and murder. Your ability to plan and react quickly will keep your family safe in the event of a home invasion.

AS SOP, the first step is to prevent the home invasion:

- Make sure all doors and windows are secured with quality locks.

- The outside of your home or apartment should be well lit.

- Get and use an alarm system. Blinds and curtains to doors and doors should be drawn so criminals are unable to case your house.

- Be careful of information you put on social media as it an allow criminals to use the internet to case your house or learn your schedules.

- Dogs are often helpful at averting burglaries and home invasions.

The second step is to prepare yourself and your home for this contingency

Designate an interior room or closet to be used as a safe room. Add extra locks to the door. Store a bag in the room that has an air horn or whistle, pepper spray, a pistol with ammunition, a couple water bottles, etc. If your home has an alarm, install a panic button in this safe room. You can even keep an old cellphone that uses pay as you go minutes. If the cellular grid is down after a disaster or shift in society, handheld radios should be utilized. Make sure you have a weapon and get legitimate training on how to use it. Often a burglar will knock on a door to see if anyone is home before making entry. If the person is unknown, only an able bodied and armed person should answer the door. Use Threat profiling to assess the threat. If an unarmed or non-able-bodied person is the only person home, do not answer, but make sure the person knows you are there by turning on the TV or talking through the door. Be prepared to initiate the contingency for home invasion.

Once your area is set, conduct a rehearsal. Once you hear a possible invasion, safely secure your weapon, ensure you and your family members take the most direct path to the safe room. Make sure accountability is conducted.

Call for police or neighbors for help. If you are able bodied, you may decide to stay outside the safe room with a firearm to defend your area. Once the drill is complete, take notes of what went right, what went wrong to adjust or improve your plan?

REACT TO CAR JACKING:

CARJACKING is a crime which involves the theft of an occupied motor vehicle. Most carjacking's occur for the sole purpose of stealing the car but can also involve an abduction.

As SOP The first step is to prevent the carjacking:

- Know your operational environment and stay out of high crime areas.

- When approaching an intersection, or stuck in traffic, be observant for any suspicious people.

- Use your mirrors to maintain 360 degrees of awareness.

- Be observant of vehicles that could be following you.

- Keep your windows and doors locked at all times.

- Park in well-lit areas.

- While driving, keep your seat belt buckled.

- While sitting in a parking area, keep your seat belt unbuckled so you can exit your vehicle quickly.

Identifying a Tail

A vehicle that follows you through three turns should be considered a threat. An unknown vehicle that follows you into your driveway should be considered a threat. While driving, always have an "out". Leave sufficient room in front of your vehicle to maneuver away from a threat. You should always be able to see the rear tires of the vehicle in front of you (Bureau of Diplomatic Security). Be cautious if your vehicle is bumped from behind or if someone attempts to flag you down. These could be an attempt to stop and rob you. If you are bumped, continue to a safe public place before stopping. If you are not an able-bodied person, call 911 instead of stopping if you see a roadside emergency.

Managing the car Jacker

If you do find yourself surprised, vehicles are several ton weapons; use this weapon to escape. Keeping proper distance between you and the vehicle in front allows you to have your "out". If the attacker is at your door, turning your wheels to the left and moving will put space between you and the threat. If the attacker has a firearm and you are unable to escape, keep calm. Attackers are often only interested in the vehicle. Give them the vehicle but do not allow yourself or any children to be adducted. Once abducted, you are in a world totally controlled by the criminal. For women and children, abductions often include rape and murder. Once you have escaped the situation, move to a safe public place and call for help.

REACT TO MUGGING:

Mugging is a crime that is often carried out by one or more attackers. The intent is often to steal money or other valuables. Sometimes muggings result in murder or rape.

As SOP, the first step is to prevent mugging:

- Know your operational environment and stay out of high crime areas.

- Don't make yourself a target.

- Don't travel alone.

- Park in well-lit areas.

- Dress in a manner that doesn't attract attention. Limit flashy watches and jewelry.

- Women should consider not carrying a large purse.

- Maintain 360 degrees of awareness and be observant for any suspicious people.

- Be observant of individuals that are following and matching your pace.

- Be warry of areas that offer canalization or individuals that have positioned themselves between you and exits from areas.

- Use your profiling techniques to evaluate these possible threats.

- Always have your "out"; a safe, public place you can run towards.

During a Mugging

If you are being robbed with a weapon, stay calm. Be careful not to aggravate your attacker. A wallet or purse is not worth your life. Slowly and calmly hand over your wallet or purse. Continue to be calm and attempt to slowly back away from the threat and move toward a safe public place. Do not allow yourself or any children to be adducted. Once abducted, you are in a world totally controlled by the criminal. For women and children, abductions often include rape and murder. If the mugger attempts to abduct you, try to break his grip and run towards a safe public place. If you can't break his grip, make your body limp; it is harder to move dead weight. Attempt to grab onto any object that will make it harder for him to move you. Attempt to attract bystanders and make him uncomfortable by yelling as loud as you can that "I am being attacked, help!"

If this struggler escalates into him striking or kicking, bundle yourself into a ball using your hands and arms to protect your head. Continue to yell "I am being attacked". If you are in a public place, time is on your side and the attacker will have to leave. Once you have escaped the situation, move to safe public place and call for help.

Muggers Wallet

A Muggers Wallet is a decoy that is given to a robber in the place of your real wallet. A Muggers Wallet should have a small amount of cash, several old credit cards, random photographs, random business cards, and old receipts. The cash should be mostly small denominations and one ten-dollar or twenty-dollar bill to give the illusion that he has gotten his prize. Do not have any personal identifying information in the wallet. Photographs shouldn't be of actual family members. Old receipts complete the illusion that this is an actual wallet.

REACT TO ABDUCTION:

When you are abducted you're being taken from your home, work, or other public place against your will. This is normally for the purpose or ransom, rape or murder.

As SOP, the first step is to react to the abduction:

If you are abducted, try your best to remain calm or regain your composure as soon as possible. You need to ask yourself the following important questions and act.

- How many are involved in the abduction?

- Use the Human Description Report and memorize the descriptions.

- What is your abductors emotional state?

- Where are you being taken?

Location and Motive

If you are blindfolded, make mental notes of the turns and times to try and have an idea of where you are being taken. If taken to other locations, be observant for exits, communication devices, and any other tools for escape.

Try and ascertain the motive for the abduction. In foreign countries, the possibility exists that you are being held for ransom. More often than not in the United States the motivation involves robbery and sexual assault. Regardless stay positive and attempt to gain rapport with your captive. Humanize yourself by keeping calm and maintaining dignity by not begging or crying.

Rapport and Rescue

Building rapport and humanizing yourself can make it harder for an abductor to cause harm. Ask for small favors to further humanize yourself and condition your abductor into providing care. Continue to assess the situation and look for a way to escape or call for help. If help does come, lay on the ground as flat and as still as you can so you do not present yourself as a threat to your rescuers.

REACT TO ACTIVE SHOOTER:

An active shooter situation is described as one or more shooters killing indiscriminate targets normal in a public, educational or business setting. These situations are unpredictable and evolve quickly.

As SOP, the first step is to avoid the shooter

Active shooter events are often short lived. The national average is 15-20 minutes from the time of the first shot. This means your early decision making will make all the difference.

RUN

- Your best option in an active shooter situation will be to run

- Look for the nearest exit

- Don't worry about personal belongings

- Don't let others slow you down

- Once safely outside call the police

- Prevent others from entering the building if possible.

HIDE

- If you cannot run because the shooter is too close you must hide

- Look for a room with a locking door

- If there are no locks barricade the door

- Shut the blinds

- Silence your cell phone

- Remain quiet and still until you are certain the shooter has left your immediate area

- Do not open the door for anyone unless provide **physical** proof that they are police

FIGHT

- If there is nowhere to hide you must fight

- Improvise weapons

- Use chairs, pens, glass, books, staplers, hole punches and anything else that can inflict bodily harm

- Surprise the attacker, you know where they are they don't know where you are

- Strike vital points like eyes, nose, throat, groin or hand holding the weapon

- Be loud and viscous catch the shooter off guard

- As soon as you can escape do so quickly, don't be a hero

Reacting to police

When the police arrive, they will have one goal and that will be to stop the shooter. They will not be able to help with first aid or let anyone else in the building to treat the injured until the shooter is stopped. Do not interfere with police. Remember, they have no idea who the shooter is and will be on high alert.

If you are approached by police or exit the building and approach them yourself be sure to put your hands up and spread your fingers. Follow their directions and be sure not to make any sudden movements.

THE SURVIVAL GROUP

Long term survival as a singleton is possible, but not ideal. Security comes first and numbers aid security. Numbers also allow personnel to split tasks effectively and allow members to become experts in their specialty. Survival groups can be centralized or decentralized. A centralized group would occupy a small area. The best example of this would be a farm in which all members of the group live. A decentralized group would live in separate houses or farms that could mutually support in a time of need. The main advantage of a centralized group is the added security permitted. The main advantage of a decentralized group is space; living in small groups, in small confines, can cause issues. An ideal situation would be a small centralized group that cooperates with other small centralized groups. Experience living in small outposts suggests that a centralized group should be a minimum of 10 able body personnel with an ideal number being closer to 30. Personnel should have a clear idea what their duty and responsibilities are.

The Group Leader is ultimately responsible for the group and provides the overarching vision. For the group to be successful, the leader must have personnel to help him manage the group. Each of these managers need to be, or become, subject matter experts in their field and more importantly cross-train the group to spread that knowledge.

GROUP SECTIONS AND RESPONSIBILITIES

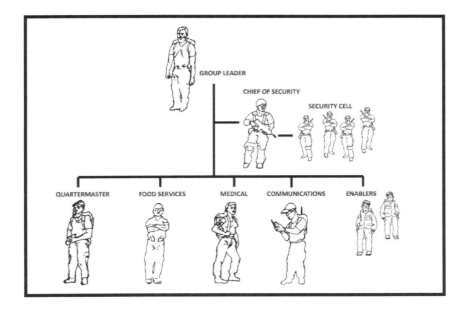

GROUP LEADER: The Group Leader is just that, the leader and responsible for everything that is good or bad. Leadership is defined as the process of directing the actions of others toward the accomplishment of a common objective. A successful leader provides vision and involves the group in the decision-making process when possible. A successful leader leads by example; leading by example is the first step in enforcing behavior and standards. A successful leader also realizes that he does not have all the answers and works to build and develop a competent group core.

CHIEF OF SECURITY: The Chief of Security reports directly to the Group Leader, and serves as the second in command. Under the Chief of Securities direct supervision is the Security Cell. Prepares and briefs members and develops equipment load plans and task organizes movements.

QUARTERMASTER: Supervises all supply actions for the group. Focal point for supply needs. Consults with all other sections and creates a complete list of the group's supply needs. Develops a system to track group supplies. Cross-trains members on cache and storage techniques.

FOOD SERVICES CHIEF: Plans, organizes, and evaluates the preparedness of the groups dietetics and food storage program. Develops and maintains proficiency in food preparation, food storage, food storage equipment, food safety, and individual dietary needs. Oversees, advises, and cross-trains group members in all aspects of dietary preparedness.

MEDICAL: Checks, inspects, and prepares groups medical supplies and equipment. Stores special medical supplies based on known needs of the group and ensures all medical equipment and supplies are properly packed. Ensures all members IFAK are to standard and cross-trains in basic medical skills.

COMMUNICATIONS: Prepares and implements the groups communication pace plan. Ensures that all member have training on all radios systems used. Determines the need for spare parts and stores these items. Obtains and maintains ham radio operator license. Keep group informed on date on digital and cyber security.

ENABLERS: Enablers are the collection of other personnel with special abilities and skillsets that provide support to your group. Some examples of enablers would be; farmers, ranchers, electricians, mechanics, plumbers, welders, blacksmiths, armorer, intelligence.

IDENTIFYING POTENTIAL GROUP MEMBERS

Attracting the right members for your group is critical. You should have an idea of your gaps or any redundancies needed. Identify these gaps and consider prospects with current employment using the skill-sets needed or access to equipment and supplies. The following are some considerations for prospective members;

- Can the prospect be trusted to keep details of the group private? Can their family be trusted to keep the details private?

- Does the individual have morals and value set similar to your group?

- What skill-sets or equipment will the prospect bring?

- What is the age and health of the prospects and their immediate family?

- How many family members does the prospect have and would this be a benefit or a hindrance?

- Does the prospect have the time and/or resources to be a contributing member?

- How close does the prospect live? If the distance is considerable, can a communication and a link-up plan be established?

The first consideration should always be security, in this case OPSEC. Can the prospects and their family keep the group's details private? Things to watch out for on social media is too much loose personal or political talk. Not having a social media account in today's age will raise more flags than having one, just make sure your potential member appears to fit the social norm. Some of this can be mitigated by not telling family members of your involvement.

Building a group that has a similar set of core values is important. In normal circumstances, differences of political and/or religious views are not a bad thing. During times of high stress, these differences will cause conflict. Conflict is a normal, yet unhealthy, way of handling stress. There will be plenty of internal dynamics, try not adding to it.

When considering a prospects skill-sets and resources, remember "troops to task". Your prospect has to have a purpose that adds rather than drains to the whole of the group. Does the individual have medical experience? If your group needs a Communication Chief, is there a local ham radio operator? Does a neighbor have heavy equipment that can be used to create obstacles? Do you know a farmer, a mechanic? Identify gaps in your group and seek to fill them.

As for age and health, this should be a consideration, not exclusion. What steps can you take to mitigate these considerations? If your Communications Chief has diabetes, can it be managed by your medic? A plan, with preparation, will keep considerations from becoming burdens.

All the members needed for your perfect group may not be within your local area. As with health considerations, can a plan be created to overcome distance? Is it possible to store some of the individual's food supplies at a fellow member's location or in a local cache? Are there multiple routes and hold up areas that can be specified and easily identified? Caches and routes will be covered in following chapters.

Lastly, what if you identify a person who doesn't believe in preparedness but has skills needed to round out your group's capabilities. Maybe it's not even worth approaching this individual. Some examples of this would be a Doctor from your community or Farmer with access to land and equipment. One option is adding them into your plan without their knowledge. Storing extra standard rations for these individuals could be a relatively cheap investment for an added skill-sets or equipment.

PERSONAL GEAR

As we discussed in Threat Profiling, styles and colors of clothing advertise to the world who we are. This should be considered when selecting our clothing. Our goal is to be the gray man.

What is the Gray Man?

The gray man blends into his environment whatever that may be. The grey man is constantly accessing his environment and seeks to look and act like the majority. If 80% of the people in his environment looks and acts a certain way, the grey man does as well within reason. The reason for wanting to be the gray man is to not present yourself as memorable or in our case someone to target/ victimize. Advertising yourself as a prepper opens yourself up for being targeted. Advertising yourself as extremely poor could also open yourself up for victimization. Again, our goal is to blend in with the majority of the population. We do not wear items like jewelry or expensive watches that targets you for theft. Avoid wearing clothing with visually distinctive slogans or symbols that allows you to be easily remembered. During a shift in society, the appearance of people will also most likely change with time.

So, what are appropriate items to wear? Pants should be khaki work pants, or blue jeans. Shirts can be anything from t-shirts to even colored polo shirts. Colors should be neutral or dark colors but blend in with local styles. Wearing camouflage or other martial clothing is outside social norms and presents yourself as a threat, and of interest to criminals or government authorities. In Afghanistan, many mujahedeen wore traditional civilian clothing in these neutral colors and were able to fight in the mountains and then quickly blend into the local villages. The same was true with Iraqi insurgents utilizing civilian clothing in urban areas. Camouflage has its place, but more often than not, neutral civilian clothing holds the advantage of being able to blend in. That being considered, clothing should be conducive for operation in the environment. Considerations include temperature, UV light, and precipitation. Shoes should also be area and temperature appropriate yet comfortable to run or walk long distances in. Tennis shoes or broken in hiking shoes work well. Backpacks should also be neutral as well. Flip flops should be avoided for obvious reasons. Try to avoid military or camouflage bags; there are many civilian options available that will allow you to blend in.

24 HOUR BAG

A 24-Hour Bag is small and purpose built for basic defense, navigation, communication, and includes limited provisions. The intent is to be smaller, discrete and easier to grab in an emergency where you have to immediately escape and would not have the time to grab the larger and more substantial 72 Hour Bag. Do not over pack.

24 HOUR BAG CONTENTS

- DEFENSE (AREA SPECIFIC; KNIFE, PISTOL, EXTRA MAGAZINES, ETC.)
- COMPASS/SMALL GPS/MAP
- VHF/UHF RADIO/CELLULAR PHONE
- SMALL FLASH LIGHT
- CASH/CREDIT CARD
- IFAK
- LIGHTER
- WATER PURIFICATION TABS
- WATER BOTTLE X2
- ENERGY BAR X2

KNOW HOW TO USE EVERYTHING IN YOUR BAG.

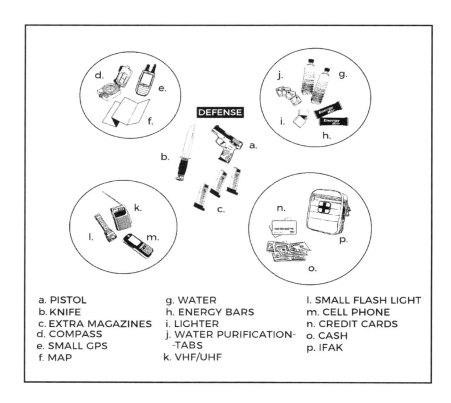

a. PISTOL
b. KNIFE
c. EXTRA MAGAZINES
d. COMPASS
e. SMALL GPS
f. MAP

g. WATER
h. ENERGY BARS
i. LIGHTER
j. WATER PURIFICATION-
   -TABS
k. VHF/UHF

l. SMALL FLASH LIGHT
m. CELL PHONE
n. CREDIT CARDS
o. CASH
p. IFAK

72 HOUR BAG

A 72 Hour Bag is a kept within your home or vehicle and is purpose built for defense, navigation, communication, extended survival, and provides 72 hours of provisions. Think of this as your emergency lifeline, your last resort. The following page has a checklist. Assemble your bag area and climate specific. Do not over pack. Your bag needs to stay manageable in size and weight. Using a frameless bag, pack no more than 25% of your body weight. When using a bag with a frame, pack no more than 40% of your body weight. Your bag and individual items need to be waterproof and sealed. Small items, extra magazines, socks, etc. can be individually vacuum sealed. Have water and 72 hours' worth of provisions. MRE's entrees are preferred over freeze-dried meals as they require no preparation. Water stored in canteens get stale but canteens are better to retrieve water with. Pack empty canteens along with six sealed bottles of water. Have three different ways to start a fire and purify water. Your water filter should be able to filter pathogens to .02 Microns. Carry an eyedropper of bleach (1 drop per 32 ounces of water). Shelter can vary from a simple tarp to a four-season tent. Assemble a small fishing and snare kit.

72 HOUR BAG CONTENTS

SECURITY
- ❑ WEAPON
- ❑ SELF DEFENSE KNIFE
- ❑ BASIC LOAD

NAVIGATION
- ❑ MAPS
- ❑ COMPASS
- ❑ GPS
- ❑ NOTEBOOK/PEN

COMMUNICATIONS
- ❑ VHF/UHF RADIO
- ❑ SHORTWAVE RADIO
- ❑ STROBE LIGHT
- ❑ SIGNAL KIT

SURVIVAL
- ❑ IFAK
- ❑ CANTEENS X2
- ❑ WATER
- ❑ 72 HOURS FOOD
- ❑ CANTEEN/FLATWARE
- ❑ WATER PURIFICATION X3
- ❑ FIRESTARTER X3
- ❑ SURVIVAL KNIFE
- ❑ POCKET CHAINSAW
- ❑ CORDAGE
- ❑ FLASH LIGHT X2
- ❑ SUNDRY PACK
- ❑ CASH/CREDIT CARD
- ❑ EXTRA SET CLOTHES
- ❑ HIKING BOOTS
- ❑ SOCKS X2
- ❑ RAIN JACKET
- ❑ SLEEPING BAG
- ❑ SHELTER
- ❑ APPLICABLE WEATHER GEAR
- ❑ FISHING/SNARE KIT

KNOW HOW TO USE EVERYTHING IN YOUR BAG

FIREARMS SELECTION

An always contested conversation is which type of firearm or caliber is the "best". The question should not be what the best is, but what is the most prevalent cartridges and weapons in your area and group to ensure that your armory matches. The most prevalent centerfire cartridges in the United States is the 9×19mm Parabellum (9mm) and 5.56×45mm (.223) NATO. Both are used by the United States military and members of the North Atlantic Treaty Organization. Furthermore, these calibers are used by the majority of local and federal agencies in the United States as well as numerous civilian sport enthusiasts. Some close seconds in centerfire pistol cartridges include the .45 ACP, .40 S&W. Close seconds in centerfire rifle cartridges include the 7.62x51mm NATO (308) and .30-06 Springfield.

So, what is the most prevalent centerfire pistol and rifle in the United States? According to the National Rifle Association, the most prevalent rifle in the United States is the AR-15. The most prevalent pistol is a little harder to identify but most likely M1911 largely because it was the standard US sidearm for over 70 years. The most prevalent pistol in *use* today is most likely the Glock 17/19 series which uses the 9x19mm Parabellum.

Additionally, many local and federal agencies are transitioning back into the 9mm variants of the Glock from the previous .40 S&W.

Having weapons standardized in your survival group does enhance your abilities, but it is not mission critical. It is more important to effectively and confidently use your firearms than to be able to share magazines or parts. That said, standardized equipment in general is something to work towards. The recommendation for a standardized pistol and rifle is the Glock 19 and an AR15 variant.

The Glock 19 is a semiauto pistol first introduced in 1990 and is chambered in the popular 9x19mm. This pistol uses Glock's Safe Action and has a standard trigger pull of 5.5lbs. With a barrel length of 4.5", the overall size of the pistol is just under that of a typical full-size pistol. This size allows it to serve as a duty pistol or concealed carry. Standard magazines capacity is 15 rounds. The Glock 19 can also use Glock 17 magazines which hold 17 rounds. Most generations of Glock 19 pistols have a rail mount for weapons lights. Night sights can also be mounted.

The AR15 has been in service with the United States Armed Forces since 1959. The AR15 is a semiauto rifle chambered in the popular 5.56×45mm NATO and uses direct gas impingement. A typical barrel length is 16" and typical magazine capacity is 30 rounds. The AR15 rifle is modular and easily customized. A book could be written on all the variants, manufacturers, calibers, and aftermarket parts. A standard 16" rifle has an effective range of 400-500 meters while precision rifle versions can be effective over 700 meters. Picatinny rails are standard or can be added to most models which allows the ability to mount weapons lights and optics.

FIREARM SAFETY

No matter if you are 100% familiar with guns and been around them your whole life you always make sure it is unloaded. If you are new to guns and unfamiliar that is ok. You need to make your main focus on learning the mechanics of your primary weapon you will be using. Remember guns are of course dangerous, but if they are handled appropriately they will not cause an incident.

GUN SAFETY STEPS

1. When you first pick up a gun, make sure to point it in a safe direction

2. Make sure the gun does not have any bullets in the chamber. And make sure if it has a safety button that you put it on safe.

3. NEVER touch the trigger until you are ready to shoot your gun.

4. If you are not planning on using the gun, do not load ammo or put the magazine in the magazine well.

1. **PISTOLS—SEMI-AUTO---** With a semi-auto pistol you need to familiarize yourself with this weapon. If it has a

safety switch, switch it to safe. Some pistols will have a red dot, if you see the red dot, this means your pistol is on fire. It can be very dangerous and deadly if mishandled. With a semi-auto, you need to first take the ammo magazine out of the magazine well. Second, you need to slide the slide to the rear and lock it in place. Physically look and make sure there is not a round in the chamber. Never stick your finger from the top down towards the magazine well or the barrel. If you do this and your slide somehow engages, it will do damage to your finger.

2. **PISTOLS---REVOLVERS---** Revolvers most likely will never have a safety switch. You must familiarize yourself with your revolver and practice when it is fully unloaded. Cocking the hammer back and slowly releasing it forward is a good way to practice when unloaded. This is something you MUST learn if you want to handle a revolver. You have to know how to slowly ride the hammer forward if you cocked it back and do not have to fire. What you do is you hold pressure on the hammer of the revolver and squeeze and hold the trigger in. While doing so keep the pressure on the hammer until you bring it forward into the original resting position.

3. **BOLT-ACTION RIFLES---**Bolt action rifles may seem a little easier after the pistols we talked about. With a bolt

action rifle, you open the bolt and look to make sure there is not a round in the chamber. With the bolt slid to the rear, this gun cannot fire, but you must always treat it as a loaded gun.

4. **SEMI-AUTO RIFLES**--- If you have a semi-auto rifle you do about the same thing. Make sure you put the safety switch on safe first as well on this gun. You first drop the magazine and pull the bolt back to the rear where you can see into the chamber. At this point, you should have locked your bolt back to the rear. You can visually verify that your gun does not have any bullets in the chamber.

5. **BREAK OPEN & SINGLE SHOT**---Now make sure that you put the safety switch on safe once again before handling the gun. If it is a single action rifle, shotgun or an over-under shotgun you will "break the barrel" open. Once you do this, you can see if there is a bullet in the chamber. Once you verify that the barrel is empty, you can do what you want with it as long as you keep it pointed in a safe direction.

HOME DEFENSE PLAN

Like individual security, creating a home and area defense plan does not only include physical preparation, it also includes building a set of habits. This plan must utilize concentric rings of security. Concentric rings of security can also be referred to as a layered defense or even described as similar to the different layers of an onion. At the center of this onion is the individual people included in the plan. The set of habits and standards discussed in the physical security is your first and last line of defense.

Moving outward, the next layers of this security include the physical security of your structure. Each building should have a designated safe haven that family or group members can retreat to in a time of emergency. As discussed previously, this safe haven should have extra locks on the door. A bag containing an air horn or whistle, pepper spray, a pistol with ammunition, water, and a method of communication should be located in the safe haven.

Bedroom doors can be reinforced by one of several aftermarket door protection kits that strengthens the hinges and jams against kicking and prying. Adding this layer could give you the seconds needed to wake and respond to an intruder that has entered your home. A firearm or other suitable item personal protection should always be available in the bedroom. A monitor for any security camera system you have is also value added in this area.

Most buildings have multiple entry doors and windows and pose a risk to break ins. Exterior door should be steel with added door protection kits. Window can be protected by security film or security bars. It is impossible to stop all break ins; the goal is to slow the intruders down so there is time to react. Locking doors must become a habit that all family or group members abide by. That one time a family member forgets to lock up could be the one time that it was truly needed.

Lighting around the home should be utilized. All entryways should be well lit. Shrubs and bushes should be cut back to limit the ability of would be criminals to hide around the house. The transition between moving from your vehicle into your house is a very vulnerable time. Always have a means of personal protection during this transition. Take that split second before exiting the vehicle to observe any suspicious activity or if anything is out of place.

Other layers that can be utilized are dogs, security camera systems, driveway alarms, and exterior fences and gates. Anything added to your home defense plan can add those valuable seconds needed to react.

The one word that I can give you as a key to success in everything you do is rehearsals. Ensure your family or group rehearse the plan. When you rehearse these plans, don't worry if all doesn't go as planned or gaps are identified. It is better to have these issues during the practice portion to adjust the overall plan.

PREPARATIONS SECURITY

Though most of what you store may be in the pantry you should also consider hiding some food. When it comes to food storage you are planning to use this food when the shelves have gone bare at the grocery store and a disaster has crippled normal circumstance.

That said you need a plan that is twofold when it comes to security

- To reinforce your home and the areas where food is stored

- To hide some food, incase desperate people are successful in penetrating your home and robbing you

As previously discussed, reinforcing the home is not all about bigger locks and bars on windows. You are primarily looking to make your home less appealing than the others on the block.

VISITORS

Though home invasion is one thing, having visitors could present future threats. The people who you work with today may become desperate monsters following a truly cataclysmic disaster. You must be very careful when you invite people into your home. Be careful what you show them and what they show themselves.

If you have food storage in several places in the home, you may just want to keep people out of that section. If they are decent people, they will respect your wishes with no questions asked. Another very helpful method of protecting your food storage from visitors is hiding the food in plain sight.

Here are several locations for food storage in your home right now:

- Box Spring

- Inside your Couch

- Cut the bottoms out of your floor level cabinets

- Hollow doors can hold dry food

- Behind smaller books on bookshelves

- Inside the walls

Beyond these places, you can also construct various false bottoms or false floors for storage of your food stuffs in plain sight.

AREA DEFENSE

Concentric rings of security extend out into your area defense. During an emergency or a shift in society, it may be necessary to establish security positions. Square, triangular, pentagon and freeform security perimeters were constructed by the early SF units in Vietnam. Through trial and some error, the triangle shape was found to be the most advantageous. The triangle provides that 360-degree security with the least amount of positions. One of these positions should be the main entry and exit point to your camp. An alternate access to the camp should also be located with another position. Positions should be placed in a location advantageous to view the largest amount of terrain while interlocking with the other two positions. These positions can be outbuildings or individually constructed. As time and recourse permit, increase the position security with sandbags and overhead cover when applicable. It is preferable to man these positions with two personnel but at times this is not available. One guard per position is acceptable if there is one additional roving guard that continually rotates through the positions. The group's largest weapon system should be placed at the most likely avenue of approach.

Obstacles should also be incorporated in the plan. A minimum of two layers of wire fencing should be stretched between these positions. Ensure the area outside your perimeter is cleared to ensure good observation and fields of fire. Any major routes into your area should also have these obstacles. These obstacles can be expedient, just try and limit items that can be used as cover or concealment for any adversary. Heavy equipment can be also used to create barriers or zones that channelize personnel.

Active Patrols are a major part of your area defense plan. During Katrina, neighborhoods banded together to create defensive positions for area security as well as these active patrols. If manning isn't available for these patrols, hidden listening and observation posts can be utilized.

If part of decentralized group that live in separate houses or farms that mutually support in a time of need, a communications net should be established. MURS base stations (Multi-Use Radio Service) should be utilized for this intermediate distance communications. Agric Alert, a similar system, was used extensively during the Rhodesia Bush Wars with good effect.

RED, WHITE, AND BLUE

We also need a series of signals to indicate if the camp or area is safe. We will use a RED, WHITE, and BLUE plan.

RED: This is the signal that the area isn't safe. This could be a streamer on the route into your base camp, a red signal left at the area or a word used verbally via radio or other means.

WHITE: The primary rally point used, to assemble or reassemble the Group for further contingency actions. The word "WHITE" will be used as the designation to specify which rally point to use. A white streamer can also be left on the route into the area or left at the camp after everyone leaves.

BLUE: The alternate rally point used, to assemble or reassemble the Group for further contingency actions. The word "BLUE" will be used as the designation for the rally point. A blue streamer can also be left on the route into the area or left at the camp after everyone leaves.

Under normal conditions; when the group is intact, it will occupy the rally point in a defensive posture, IAW security halts procedures. The senior Group member to arrive will establish a security perimeter and begin accountability of all personnel who have arrived and those arriving.

BASE DEFENCE RULES

- A DETAILED COPY OF THE BASE DEFENSE PLAN WILL BE POSTED IN THE BRIEFING AREA AND ALL GROUP PERSONELL WILL HAVE A UNDERSTAND THE PLAN.

- BASE DEFENSE WILL BE REHEARSED ON A REGULAR BASIS, ESPECIALLY IF CHANGES HAVE BEEN MADE TO THE PLAN.

- ALL REHEARSALS WILL BE BRIEFED (INCLUDING TIME) TO THE TEAM PRIOR TO HAPPENING AS TO AVOID ANY CONFUSION BETWEEN A REHEARSAL AND AN ACTUAL ATTACK.

- ALL TEAM MEMBERS WILL HAVE A SMALL RED LENSE LIGHT ON THEIR KIT FOR NIGHT RECONITION.

- THE MOST CASUALTY PRODUCING WEAPONS WILL BE PLACED AT THE MOST VULNERABLE POINTS AND MOST LIKELY POINTS OF ATTACK.

- OBSTACLES, EARLY WARNING SYSTEMS, AND ADDITIONAL COVER WILL BE EMPLACED. (METT-C DEPENDENT).

- POSITIONS WILL COMBINE TO PROVIDE 360 DEGREE SECURITY AND INTERLOCKING SECTORS OF FIRE.

- TOC AND KEY LOCATIONS WILL HAVE YELLOW CHEMLIGHTS HUNG FOR EMERGENCY LIGHTING. MEDICAL SHED WILL HAVE RED CHEMLIGHTS AVAILABLETO BE HUNG OUTSIDE THE ENTRANCE.

- LOADED MAGAZINES AND EXTRA AMMO FOR ALL WEAPONS SYSTEMS WILL BE PLACED IN THE OPCEN AND DEEMED AS FORCE PRO AMMO. THIS AMMO IS TO BE USED ONLY FOR BASE DEFENSE SITUATIONS AND NOT TO BE USED FOR TRAINING OR RELOADING AFTER MISSION.

- SMALL ARMS WILL NOT BE LEFT UNATTENDED.

- ADDITIONAL WEAPONS WILL BE PLACED IN THE OPCEN TO BE USED AS BACK-UPS OR WHEN METT-C REQUIRES.

- PERSONNEL WILL BE IDENTIFIED FOR AN ASSAULT TEAM THAT WILL BE USED AT THE DISCRETION OF LEADERSHIP

- ALL ENTRY POINTS WILL BE LOCKED AT NIGHTFALL.

- PERSONELL WILL ROTATE GUARD SHIFTS THROUGHOUT THE DAY AND NIGHT IN ORDER TO MAINTAIN SECURITY.

- BASE PERIMETER WILL BE INSPECTED REGULARLY AND IMPROVEMENTS MADE IF NEEDED.

- PERSONNEL WILL BE ARMED AT ALL TIMES, AT A MINIMUM CARRYING A PISTOL.

- NO OUTSIDERS WILL BE ALLOWED ON BASE WITH A WEAPON DURING BASE DEFENSE DRILLS, CHILDREN AND ELDERLY WILL BE MOVED AND SECURED IN THE SAFE HAVEN. A DETAIL WILL BE CREATED TO ENSURE THEY ARE MOVED AND ACCOUNTED FOR.

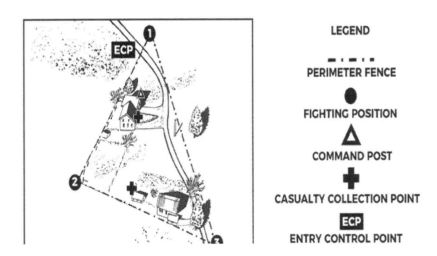

LEGEND

- - · - · - PERIMETER FENCE

● FIGHTING POSITION

△ COMMAND POST

✚ CASUALTY COLLECTION POINT

ECP ENTRY CONTROL POINT

MISSION PLANNING

When planning an undertaking, the leader should use the following procedures to aid in planning and executing your assigned missions or complicated efforts.

STEP 1. DETERMINE THE MISSION: The leader may receive a mission or tasking from a group leader or determine the need for a mission themselves. The first consideration for planning is time. The leader should use no more than one third of the available time for his own planning and for issuing of the complete plan. Considerations like time for pack out, rehearsals, equipment prep, and travel time should be factored in.

STEP 2. ISSUE A WARNING ORDER. The leader provides initial instructions to the group in a warning order. The warning order contains enough information for group members to begin preparations and mirrors the five -paragraph OPORD format.

The following information may be included in a warning order.

- The mission or nature of the task.

- Time and place for the mission brief.

- Who is taking part in the mission?

- The timeline for the mission.

- Any special instructions that need to be attended to immediately.

STEP 3. MAKE A TENTATIVE PLAN. Make an initial plan using the following considerations outlines in the factors of **METT-TC**:

(1) Mission. Review the mission to ensure you fully understand all tasks.

(2) Enemy. Consider the enemy and environmental threats in the area. Identify the greatest threats to the mission and then determine how you can counter or nullify those threats.

(3) Terrain. Consider the effects of terrain and weather using **O**bservation, **C**oncealment, **O**bstacles, **K**ey terrain, and **A**venues of approach **(OCOKA)**.

(4) Troops available. Consider the number of group members on the mission, the characteristics of your available weapons and how this will affect each portion of your mission.

(5) Time available. Reevaluate the time available based on the initial plan.

(6) Civilian considerations. Consider the impact of the local population.

STEP 4. START NECESSARY MOVEMENT. Depending on your reevaluated time considerations, it may be necessary to begin movement to a forward staging area prior to the completion of the entire plan.

STEP 5. RECONNOITER. At a minimum, leaders will make a map reconnaissance or rely on individuals who have first-hand knowledge of the area. It is preferable for the leader to make personal reconnaissance.

STEP 6. COMPLETE THE PLAN. Once we consider METT-C and conduct the reconnaissance, we can complete the plan. If time allows, **Course of Action Development** can be used to identify a plan with a high probability of success. Once the plan is complete, review to ensure it meets the original intent.

STEP 7. ISSUE THE COMPLETE PLAN. Brief the plan to the group ensuring that all understand the intent, mission specific tasks, routes, and individual assignments of all involved. Specific examples of briefs are included for mounted and dismounted operations. Use photographs, maps, and terrain models to brief the plan. The complete order can also be briefed from a concealed position within sight of the objective.

STEP 8. SUPERVISE. Once the plan is briefed, the leadership is responsible for conducting rehearsals and pre-mission inspections. Both rehearsals and pre-mission inspections are key to mission success and should not be skipped. Remember, the first step involves factoring these in to ensure they are completed.

COURSE OF ACTION DEVELOPMENT

Course of action (COA) development and analysis is arguably the most important part of developing options and selecting the best plan for mission success. The group should have a wide variety of backgrounds and experience that aids in developing solid COA's. Plainly put, many heads are better than one. Group members will be split into three groups to further develop their assigned COA ensuring they meet the following principles.

SUITABLE: Does it accomplish the mission?

FEASIBLE: is the group capable of accomplishing this mission? Is the group trained? Does it require special skills?

ACCEPTABLE: do the benefits outweigh the risks?

DISTINGUISHABLE: is there significant differences between COA's?

COMPLETE: each COA should have a graphic, task organization, and basic medical and communications plan.

Once the three COA's have been developed, a decision matrix will be built using the scored following criteria. Each COA is briefed by its representative and scored by the group 1 to 5. It is important for group members to be unbiased during scoring of the COA's.

COURSE OF ACTION CRITERIA

SURPRISE: least chance of enemy compromise throughout mission.

SURVIVABILITY: ability to survive operational conditions, enemy contact.

SIMPLICITY: less moving parts, complexity, fewer uncontrolled factors.

FLEXIBILITY: transition to react to new developments.

SPEED: time required for completing movement and mission.

LOGISTICALLY SUSTAINABLE: suitable use of supplies.

After all COA's are briefed and scored, the final results are reviewed and the final decision is made by the group leadership. Often the final plan includes details of one or all COA's.

CRITERIA	COA 1	COA 2	COA 3
SURPRISE			
SURVIVABILITY			
SIMPLICITY			
FLEXIBILITY			
SPEED			
SUSTAINABLE			
TOTAL			

PLANNING FORMAT

1. Situation

    A. Enemy: **S**ize, **A**ctivity, **L**ocation, **U**nit ID, **T**ime, **E**quipment **(SALUTE)**

    B. Friendly: Friendly locations, personalities in the area of operation.

2. Mission: Who, What, When, Where, Why **(5 W's)**

3. Execution:

    A. Missions Intent:

    B. Mission Overview: A brief six sentence overview of the total operation. All mission essential tasks will be briefed.

    C. Maneuver: This portion explains in detail, the mechanics of the operation. The most important part of the mission is identified. All personnel and tasks, related to the main effort, are identified also.

    D. Coordinating Instructions

- o Order of Movement/Formations for Movement to be used

- o Departure and reentry of camp

- o Security Assignments during: Movements/Halts

- o Route to the Objective: (Primary and Alternate)

- o Rally Points:

- o Actions at Danger Areas

- o Contingencies: Actions on Enemy Contact

4. Support:

A. Logistics:

- o Food: (Not only what taken on the mission, but any other availability in area)

- o Water: (Not only what taken on the mission, but any other availability in area)

- o Special Equipment: additional equipment needed for movement, mission, etc

B. Medical:

- o Location of medical supplies

- o Designated medics

- o Medical locations (closest during each portion of mission)

5. Command and Signal:

A. Communications Plan:

- o **PACE**

B. Contact Windows:

C. Callsigns and Visual Signals to be used:

D. Command: Chain of command and their location during mission

DISMOUNTED OPERATIONS

The following describes the movement techniques and formations to be used by the Group during field and tactical operations. The Group will select movement techniques based on METT/C. The Patrol Leader must place himself where he can best control the Group. Personnel breakdown will vary in accordance with number of, personnel assigned.

The distance between personnel varies according to the terrain and enemy. Each patrol member is responsible for a different sector to provide all-round security while on the move. Leaders direct movement by using arm-and-hand signals. Radios should be used only as a backup means of communicating.

The teams are split into two groups for security; Alpha Team and Bravo Team. This SOP will be based on an 8-person team but can be scaled up or down as needed. The overall principle of movement is Alpha Team leads and Bravo team is utilized for security, support by fire, and flanking maneuvers.

FORMATIONS

FILE FORMATION: Used in restrictive terrain, dense foliage, or during periods of darkness. The patrol can rapidly form from the column formation into other formations. The column simplifies control and provides good security as long as proper dispersion between personnel is used. 15-30 feet dispersion is optimal. 5-10 feet dispersion should be used in the hours of darkness or dense terrain.

FILE FORMATION

COLUMN FORMATION: Used when traveling down roads or through urban areas and is similar to the file except it adds lateral dispersion. 15-30 feet is proper dispersion in most terrain. When traveling down roads this zig-zag pattern is used with the personnel towards the edges of the road.

COLUMN FORMATION

WEDGE FORMATION: Used in open areas and crossing linear danger areas where the tactical situation permits. This formation is used when enemy contact is possible and allows better maneuverability, command/control and frontal fires.

Typically, two separate wedges are used during a patrol with each wedge having between three and five patrol members. The front wedge (Alpha Team) and the following wedge (Bravo Team). Dispersion between personnel is dependent on terrain and visibility. 15-30 feet is proper dispersion in most terrain.

Dispersion between Alpha and Bravo Team also varies but should be between 15-50 feet. Bravo Team can be used as a maneuver element to flank around into an enemy position if contact is made. Bravo Team is also used to set in a support by fire position to cover Alpha Teams movement to a danger area or across a linear danger area.

WEDGE FORMATION

DIAMOND FORMATION

DIAMOND FORMATION

Used when traveling in small groups. Typically used when moving forward to perform reconnaissance. The diamond provides good 360-degree security. Tighter dispersion between personnel is often used. 10-15 feet dispersion is optimal. In hours of darkness or restrictive terrain, 5-10 feet dispersion can be used.

The diamond formation is also used in personal protection details and can be adapted when conducting movement with children or individuals unable to protect themselves. When this technique is utilized, additional personnel should be pushed well ahead of the formation to ensure the route is clear.

MOVEMENT TECHNIQUES

TRAVELING OVERWATCH:

Traveling Overwatch movement technique is employed when enemy contact is likely (possible). The patrol moves in the designated formation with 100 to 200 feet between elements. Both elements move continuously, following covered and concealed routes. The lead element (Alpha Team) is approximately 100 to 200 feet ahead of the trail element, depending on terrain and vegetation. The trail element (Bravo Team) moves at varying speeds, stopping as required to overwatch the lead. Visual contact is maintained with the lead element at all times. An advantage to this technique is speed, but security is decreased.

The trail element matches the leads movement at such a distance that should the enemy engage the lead element, it will not prevent the trailing element from firing or moving to support the lead element. In wooded areas or restricted terrain, the units reduce speed and interval.

BOUNDING OVERWATCH:

Bounding Overwatch is employed when enemy contact is expected. The basic movement formation is the wedge with 15-30 feet intervals between personnel. Lead element (Alpha Team) bounds forward following a covered and concealed route. The trail element (Bravo Team) covers the progress of the bounding element from covered and concealed positions offering observation and fields of fire against suspected enemy positions. Visual contact is maintained at all times. The length of a bound is based on terrain analysis and the ranges and fields of fire from the supporting element. The advantage to this technique is a high level of security but speed is sacrificed.

BOUNDING OVERWATCH

ACTIONS AT SECURITY HALTS

Listening halts will be conducted periodically during movement to detect other movement or activity and to keep our hearing trained to the surroundings. The Group will move and halt at different intervals for at least 10 to 15 minutes.

A cigar or circular shape perimeter will be established during these halts insuring 360 degrees' security has been established and maintained at all times.

Extended Halts:

Overnight halts will be conducted IAW with Group tactical operating procedures. These halts will be conducted with the purpose of resting, chow, water resupply, planning, and communication.

A patrol base, or an extended cigar shape perimeter will be established based on Group personnel capabilities. For short stays a RON stop can be made where enemy activity is minimal, and the area is dominated by thick vegetation that will restrict personnel movement during the hours of low visibility.

SECURITY HALT

HAND AND ARM SIGNALS

Hand and arm signals are one of the most common forms of communication used during patrolling and will be utilized as much as possible in accordance with noise discipline standards. These signals are a way for leaders to quietly exercise command and control over their patrol so it is imperative that all members understand each signal. Leaders of dismounted patrols will use these hand and arm signals to control the movement of both individuals and groups. These same hand and arm signals can be used to control vehicles movement formations.

AS SOP, all hand and arm signals will be given clearly.

AS SOP, each member of the formation will pass the signal on.

EXAMPLES AND DEFINITIONS OF HAND AND ARM SIGNALS:

Freeze:

1. Signal: Clinched fist.

2. Action: Stop all movement and noise immediately. This signal will be used when the member of the patrol sees, hears, or smells the

enemy or something suspicious. The first person who detects the enemy (visually or otherwise) will give the freeze hand and arm signal. Every person halts in place, weapon at the ready, and remains absolutely motionless and quiet until further signals or orders are given.

Stop:

1. Signal: Bend arm back, open hand, fingers extended and joined.

2. Action: All personnel get down on one knee and faces their security sector. When in file formation, everyone will take two steps to the side before getting down, forming a cigar shaped perimeter. This action is used when approaching enemy ground elements, or aircraft is heard in the distance and the patrol has sufficient time to seek cover and concealment

Enemy:

1. Signal: Point in the direction of enemy troops using your hand or weapon then at your eyes,

nose, or ears depending on whether you see, smell, or hear the enemy.

2. Action: Patrol stops all movement and freezes in place.

Security Halt:

1. Action: Patrol conducts a temporary security.

2. Signal: Palms down; move in a circular motion.

Speed up:

1. Signal: Bend arm at elbow. Quickly pump fist up and down.

2. Action: Patrol increases pace in accordance with man giving the signal

Linear Danger Area:

1. Signal: Draw knife edge of hand across throat.

2. Action: Patrol executes danger crossing procedures as signaled

Go Prone:

1. Signal: Motion up and down with arm (elbow locked) from shoulder level to waist.

2. Action: Patrol assumes a prone position.

Head Count:

1. Signal: Tap the top of your head with your hand.

2. Action: Last person in the patrol counts himself as one and each person adds a number forward until the total reaches the patrol leader.

Pace Count:

1. Signal: Tap your boot with your hand.

2. Action: Pace man passes the count to the PL.

Ok/Clear:

1. Signal: Thumbs up.

2. Action: Patrol continues movement.

Conduct Reconnaissance (or check it out):

1. Signal: One finger pointed to the eyes, then in the direction or area that requires reconnoitering.

2. Action: Reconnoiter area pointed to by the signaler. Give this signal to the person tasked to execute the recon and point to the location you wish him to go.

Need Patrol Leader:

1. Signal: Tap two fingers on shirt collar

2. Action: Patrol leader will move to person indicating the signal.

Line Abreast Formation:

1. Signal: Hold arms out parallel to the ground with elbows locked.

2. Action: Team will get on line with whomever is giving the signal. Usually this is used when enemy is sighted, be prepared to execute hasty ambush.

Move in a Wedge Formation:

1. Signal: Hold non-firing arm generally backwards and out, forming half of an upside down "V".

2. Action: Patrol assumes a wedge formation.

File:

1. Signal: Extend non-firing arm with elbow bent, and motion backwards and forwards as in marching.

2. Action: Patrol assumes file formation.

Rally Points:

1. Signal: Make a circular motion over your head and then point to the actual rally point.

2. Action: Each man will then pass the signal back once he reaches the designated point. The rally point is designated by the point man.

Listening Halt:

1. Signal: Take a knee, face out and take off hat.

2. Action: Each patrol member will then pass the signal back. Each patrol member will conduct SLLS (Stop, Look, Listen, Smell) for a period of no less than 5 minutes. Listening halts will be conducted before and after any linear danger area and various times through the patrol as specified by the patrol leader

FREEZE

SPEED UP

STOP

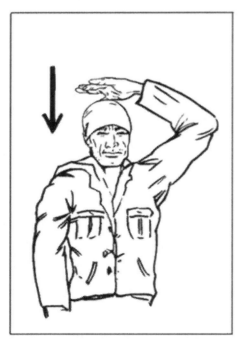

HEAD COUNT

LISTENING HALT

GO PRONE

FORM COLUMN

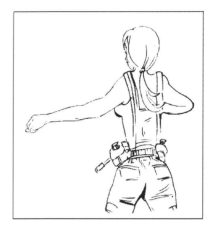

LINE ABREAST FORMATION

SECURITY HALT

RALLY POINT

LINEAR DANGER AREA

FORM FILE

FORM WEDGE

IMMEDIATE ACTION DRILLS

Immediate Action Drills (IAD's) are a set series of reactions that provide a standard and quick response to enemy contact. These drills increase survivability and can be used by numbers of personnel from two and up. This SOP will not include a total list of drills as they should be developed and tailored to your group. This SOP will include withdrawal from contact. In military operations, IAD's are often defensive and offensive in nature. A base of fire is laid and defensive positions are set. Either subsequent or simultaneous, a second element is sent to flank and attack the enemy. In a survival situation, any loss of personnel can be detrimental and cascading. Ambushes are advantageous for the enemy; the terrain and timing were chosen for a reason. During a chance contact (a contact where both sides are surprised) the terrain and numbers may or may not be advantageous for the enemy. It is still advisable to withdraw and plan an attack in a location, time, and with the numbers advantageous to your group.

HASTY AMBUSH: A hasty ambush is initiated when the patrol sees, hears or smells the enemy first, and the enemy is unaware of the patrols presence. This IAD is both a defensive measure to avoid contact and an offensive measure if the patrol is discovered. In either case, when signaled, the members of the patrol will move where indicated and take up the best available concealed firing position. If visual and physical contact can be avoided, the ambush is not initiated unless the patrol is detected. If the patrol is detected by the enemy, the first man aware of the detection will initiate the ambush by opening fire and shouting "fire." This insures initiation of the ambush if his weapon misfires.

ACTIONS ON FRONTAL CONTACT

WITHDRAW BY FIRE (WEDGE): Alpha Team drops to the ground behind cover and returns fire, Bravo Team who is further away from the contact, maneuvers to the left rear flank or right rear flank of Alpha Team to provide a base of fire. Once Bravo team is set and has begun returning fire, Alpha Team withdraws on order. These movements bounding back are situationally dependent and can be all at once or two at a time. Alpha Team will move in the opposite direction of contact approximately 50 meters past Bravo Team and establish a base of fire. After Alpha team is set and has begun returning fire, Bravo Team withdraws and all continue leap frogging away from the contact. Once out of contact a decision will be made to continue movement, return to base, or establish a hasty ambush location at an area advantageous to the group.

WITHDRAW BY FIRE (FILE): This method is used to quickly break undesired but unavoidable chance contact to the patrols front while moving in a file formation.

Immediately upon contact, each patrol member will take one or two steps to their assigned side of security, hit the ground and face the contact.

The first man in contact will fire 10-15 rounds, in the direction of the enemy, after which the weapon is placed on safe and he will turn and run down the middle of the formation to the rear of the patrol. He will continue moving in the opposite direction of the contact for approximately 50 meters, halt, and then face the contact.

The second man in the formation will fire 10-15 rounds once the first man passes his position. This will provide covering fire as the first man moves to the rear.

The third man in the formation will follow the same procedure except he will throw a smoke grenade once his 10-15 rounds are competed.

This procedure will be continued by all members of the patrol until reaching the last man the formation. The last man in the formation will throw an additional smoke grenade once he expends his 10-15 rounds.

If a weapon malfunctions during withdraw, the individual will not attempt to clear his weapon until reaching the second peel location. He will shout malfunction and immediately peel back. The next man in the formation will begin firing once the shout is heard or when the man begins to move.

Magazine changes will be conducted after each man has peeled. Other versions of the peel technique call for the dumping of a complete magazine, this adds time to your withdrawal and leaves you without a loaded weapon during a close contact.

Individuals wounded and unable to move on their own will be assisted by the closest member to him. The remainder of the patrol will provide covering fires until the wounded is moved to the rear.

ACTIONS OF FRONTAL CONTACT
(FILE)

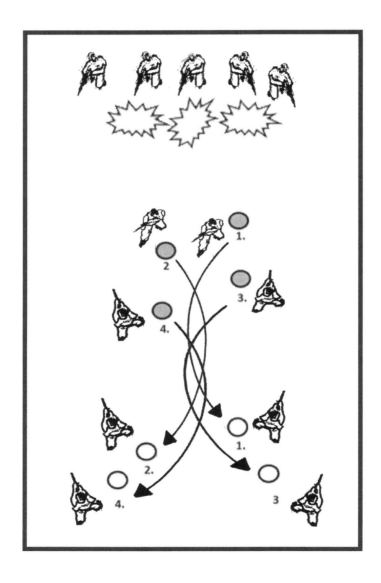

ACTIONS ON FLANK CONTACT

REACT TO FLANK CONTACT (WEDGE): Alpha Team drops to the ground behind cover and returns fire. Bravo Team who is further away from the contact, maneuvers to flank the enemy and provides a base of fire. Once Bravo team is set and has begun returning fire, Alpha Team withdraws on order. These movements bounding back are situationally dependent and can be all at once or two at a time. Alpha Team will move in the opposite direction of contact approximately 50 meters past Bravo Team and establish a base of fire. After Alpha team is set and has begun returning fire, Bravo Team withdraws and all continue leap frogging away from the contact. Once out of contact a decision will be made to continue movement, return to base, or establish a hasty ambush location at an area advantageous to the group.

REACT TO FLANK CONTACT (FILE): Flank contacts can be considered the same as ambush. Depending on the distance of the enemy's fire, appropriate actions will be taken.

Men in the kill zone, without order or signal, will immediately take cover, return fire, and perform a "**Peel Right**" or "**Peel Left**".

To conduct this peel, simultaneous to a base of fire being established, the lead man will throws a smoke towards the ambush line and turns and runs, or quickly crawls, behind the line of friendly fire to the rear of the patrol. He will continue moving to the rear direction of the patrol for approximately 50 meters, halt, then face the contact.

The second man in the formation will fire 10-15 rounds and once the first man passes his position, places his weapon on safe turns and runs behind the formation and passes the first man, halts, and faces the contact.

This procedure will be continued by all members of the patrol until reaching the last man the formation.

If a weapon malfunctions during the withdraw, the individual will not attempt to clear his weapon until reaching the second peel location. He will shout malfunction and immediately peel back. The next man in the formation will begin firing once the shout is heard or when the man begins to move.

Magazine changes will be conducted after each man has peeled.

Individuals wounded and unable to move on their own will be assisted by the closest member to him. The remainder of the patrol will provide covering fires until the wounded are moved to the rear.

Men not in the kill zone will maneuver to provide a base of fire on the enemy while members in the kill zone peel.

ACTIONS AT DANGER AREAS

LINEAR DANGER AREA

Linear Danger Areas (LDA) are most often roads. Before crossing a LDA, the patrol will halt a safe distance away from the danger area. The Alpha Team Leader will move forward and determine if it is a danger area, observe the area across the LDA to ensure it is the patrol can safely cross and continue movement.

The near side rally point will be used in the event the patrol is dispersed during enemy contact. If the last rally point that was designated is within 300 meters or less of the danger area, the previous designated RP will be used. A far side rallying point will be designated 300 meters across the danger area, on the direction of movement azimuth. Once the point man gives the signal for linear danger area;

1. Bravo Team will move up through Alpha Team to position itself to establish near side security.

2. The Alpha Team element will cross the danger area and establish far side security. The Alpha Team leader will visually ensure there is a 50-meter area or area large enough for the patrol.

3. Once cleared, Bravo Team moves across and through the security position created by Alpha Team and continues movement in the direction of travel for approximately 50 meters. Movement across will be dictated by terrain and enemy situation. **Wedge, File, On Line** or one by one can all be used. Speed is security and **Wedge** or **One Line** is preferable.

4. Once Bravo Team is set, Alpha Team moves from its far side security positions to and through the position created by Bravo Team. Once Alpha Team passes through, Bravo team picks up and all continue movement.

CROSSING A LINEAR DANGER AREA

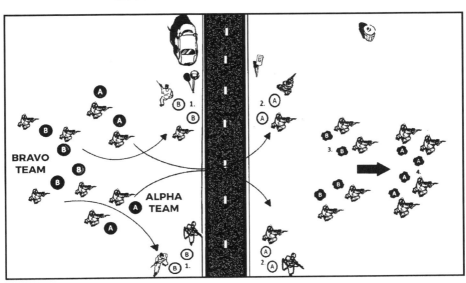

SMALL OPEN AREAS

Contour Bypass Method:

1. The patrol leader will select an identifiable reference point on the far side of the danger area that is on the same azimuth of the direction of movement.

2. The PL will then decide which side of the danger area to contour, and move the patrol by bordering the danger area.

3. Once the patrol reaches the reference point on the other side, the point man will continue on the original azimuth.

LARGE OPEN AREAS

When the patrol encounters a large open area, which cannot be bypassed, the area is negotiated same as a linear danger area. The only difference is that extra time will be used to ensure a support by fire position is properly established.

Regardless of the type of danger area or location of where the patrol makes enemy contact, they will move and assemble at the last designated rally point.

URBAN OPERATIONS

GUNFIGHTER RULES

1. Don't bring a gun, bring two.

2. Anything worth shooting once is worth shooting three times.

3. Only hits count, you can't miss fast enough to win.

4. Keep shooting until the threat no longer exists.

5. Security first; fight tunnel vision and be aware of your surroundings.

6. Use your pistol to fight to your long gun.

7. Have a plan with contingencies ready; plans don't survive first contact.

8. Flank your adversary when possible. Protect yours.

9. Watch hands, hands kill.

10. Be polite, be professional, but have a plan to kill everyone you meet.

The first point needing to be covered is that we are not assaulters. We are not rescuing hostages or storming a terrorist stronghold. We will be operating in a survival situation and moving through the urban environment in a quick, but deliberate and controlled manner.

AS SOP, WE WILL;

- MOVE THROUGH A STRUCTURE WITH A MINIMAL OF TWO PERSONNEL

- ENTER AN UN-CLEARED ROOM WITH A MINIMUM OF TWO PERSONNEL AND A MAXIMUM OF FOUR INDIVIDUALS

- PIE OFF ALL DOORS BEFORE ENTERING

- CLEAR ROOMS USING A MODIFIED STRONG WALL TECHNIQUE

- WILL NOT LEAVE YOUR POINT OF DOMINATION UNTIL "ROOM CLEAR" IS CALLED OR YOU CALL YOURSELF FORWARD TO CLEAR A "REDZONE"

- AVOID AND LIMIT TIMES INFRONT OF DOORS, WINDOWS, HALLWAYS AND

STARWELLS; THESE ARE CONCIDERED FATAL FUNNELS

At a minimum, clear a room with two personnel. With our SOP of clearing the entire door before entering, most rooms can be cleared with only two. Do not bring more than four personnel into an un-cleared room. There may be times when an individual will have to clear a structure solo. The techniques discussed below will work in one man clears but this is never preferable.

Rooms are differentiated into two basic categories, center fed room and corner fed. The key to understanding the differentiation is the placement of the door. If a door can open all the way it is safe to assume there are no walls inhibiting its movement. This would make it a center fed room. If the door stops and hits a wall when opening it is safe to assume it is a corner fed room with no additional wall.

In a military or police environment, it is preferable to use the tactic of opposing corners which create a miniature L-Shaped ambush in the room. This is accomplished in a corner fed room by the number 1 man and 2 man only taking one corner. Once all personnel are in the room, assaulters are in opposing corners and the L-Shaped ambush is achieved. In a center fed room the only change is number one man goes down two corners. By having the number one man go down to corners and all other personnel going to their respective points of domination, the same L-Shaped ambush is achieved.

For our purposes, we will clear as much of the room from the outside the room and just gain a foothold in the room by the number one man and number two man traveling down their respective walls five feet. This distance allows a foothold large enough for four personnel to enter the room. Once corners are cleared and the foothold is gained, cell members continue on line across the room. If there are any red zones, the person with the best angle to the red zone can calls themselves forward to clear, essentially the same L-Shaped ambush is achieved as in the opposing corners method in a more controlled way.

URBAN EQUIPMENT SETUP

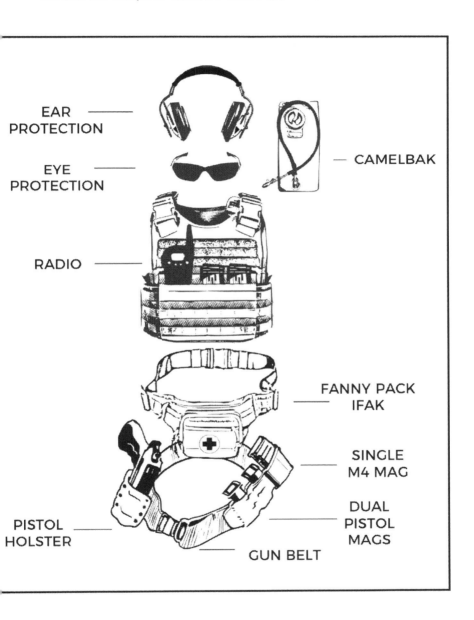

EAR PROTECTION

EYE PROTECTION

CAMELBAK

RADIO

FANNY PACK IFAK

SINGLE M4 MAG

DUAL PISTOL MAGS

PISTOL HOLSTER

GUN BELT

When setting up an urban kit, our number one priority needs to be maneuverability. We want a slim setup that allows us to effectively move in and out of vehicles, the urban environment, and most importantly allows us to effectively utilize our weapons systems. Eye and ear protection are a priority and helmets are value added. The section below will discuss the body armor and pistol belt setup.

BODY ARMOR: When selecting armor, consider using a plate carrier with ceramic plates and ballistic Kevlar backers. Different manufactures will have their ballistic ratings listed. Generally, Level III provides multi-hit protection against 7.62 mm FMJ and is sufficient and economical for our uses. When setting up the fit of the plate carrier, the plate should cover over the sternum, heart and lungs. Balance weight between the front and the back of the carrier so the front does not sag. Sagging armor will can expose the top of the heart and lungs. A radio will be somewhere on your kit that you can grab with both hands. Magazines will be stored in pouches that are closed or open top pouches with retention. Two to four magazines on our kit is sufficient. We will also have a spare mag on our belt and one in our gun. Four full magazines will give 120 rounds 5.56. This is sufficient when you consider we utilize spare mags from vehicles and fighting position before using any on our personal kit. As SOP, no pouches will be over the draw side of your pistol. It is preferable not to have pouches on your off side. Keeping the sides clean is important so nothing inhibits the drawing of your pistol or spare magazines. A tourniquet will be out and attached to your kit in a location that can be grabbed with both hands. A water reservoir will be in a pouch located on the back of your plate carrier. This helps balance out our carrier. Smaller reservoirs (35-60 ounce) are advised to keep us lite and maneuverable.

PISTOL BELT: Pistol will remain unhindered by any equipment on the draw side of the body. Holster will always have some form of retention for combat operations. On the opposite side of the pistol 2-3 pistol magazine pouches will be worn. An AR15 ready mag will be directly behind the pistol pouches. The ready mag will be your primary magazine for rifle reloads. This allows you to have a rifle mag at times you have only your pistol belt on and is faster than pulling a spare AR15 magazine from your kit. A nice to have item is a dump pouch worn behind your ready mag for spent magazines that you may occur. Your IFAK should be worn as a fanny pack and adjusted to fit comfortably with your pistol belt either in the front or back. Wearing in the front makes it easily assessable while wearing it to the rear allows lumbar support in mounted situations.

Somewhere on your kit a red chemlight will be worn. It will only be cracked in the event of a life-threatening injury so everyone else around will know that you have been wounded. A small pressure activated light should be located either on your plate carrier or belt to be pulled out for activation in low light / no light situations. Additionally, a Gerber will always be located in a place where you can get to it with both hands.

KIT BAG: Finally, you should always have a designated kit bag that holds your essential kit. Essential kit is depicted on the next page. It at the very least is your IFAK, eye and hearing protection, body armor, pistol belt, and any accessories to your rifle (lights, slings, etc). Equipment is always packed "first in, last on". Generally, your armor is packed first, then your pistol belt, followed by eye and hearing protection and IFAK. This should always be readily available. The kit bag will be the last thing loaded in vehicles so it is easily assessable.

DUTIES AND RESPONSIBILITIES OF PERSONNEL

NUMBER ONE MAN: The number one man gains as much visual knowledge on the door and breach point as possible. The number one man identifies if the door is metal or wood, if there are hinges on the outside or inside indicating it is a push door or pull door.

The number one man waits for the signal from the number two man go.

Our SOP is to squeeze the triceps muscle. The number one man will not move until he feels the squeeze. On command, the number one man clears in an arcing path around the breach clearing as much of the room as possible.

Once visually cleared or after any targets are engaged, the number one man any direction he chooses into the room and once clearing the breach faces his weapon and plates to his point of domination (the first corner). Clear this initial corner with the eyes first because they are the fastest thing on his body, then turn your body and weapon panning across the room while continuing 5 feet into the room along the wall. The number one man pans his weapon to the number two man and stops 1 meter (length of a rifle) off of his barrel. In a corner fed room number one man only goes down one corner to get to his point of domination.

DELIBERATE CLEAR OF THE BREACH

NUMBER TWO MAN: The number two man is in charge of the stack, and his primary duty is to control the number one man by holding onto the shoulder strap or shirt collar of the number one man to insure he does not try and enter the room when the assault is not ready. The number two man maintains accountability of all men, and when ready executes a signal to the number one man to

FOUR MAN ROOM POSITIONS

NOTE:

**NUMBER ONE AND TWO MEN
CLEAR THEIR CORNERS FIRST**

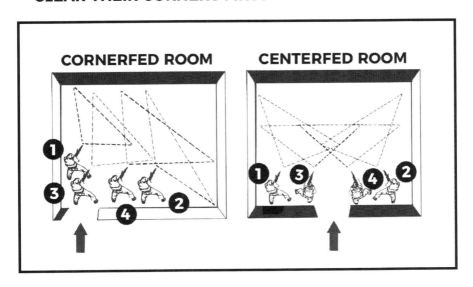

CORNERFED ROOM **CENTERFED ROOM**

move into the breach point and structure. Once the signal is given the number two man follows the one man into the breach point going the opposite direction that the number one man goes. When going to his point of domination (his corner), he immediately squares his plates and presents his rifle to the corner. He visually clears it with his eyes and simultaneously moves his body to his corner and pans his rifle across the room looking for threats until he reaches one meter (length of a rifle) off of number one man.

NUMBER THREE AND FOUR MEN: Provides security and awaits movement of the stack into the structure. Upon movement of the stack, these individuals go the opposite direction of the person in front of them and take one step into the room getting their body out of the door and pans their rifles in the direction he stepped into the room and then pans his rifle the opposite direction scanning the room for threats until he is one meter off of the other one or two man's barrels. This completes his primary and secondary sector of fire in the room.

FOLLOW ON ROOMS Upon room clear being called, all personnel can come off the wall and start moving on line across the room towards the next door. Any obstacles like open doors or un-cleared portions of the room can be dealt as the team moves across. If there are multiple open doors, team members can start plugging these doors. It is his responsibility to pie off the door and provide security for his teammates. In the event that this door is the next room to enter, this person would become number one man.

TREAT THE ENTRIES INTO HALWAYS AS YOU WOULD ANY OTHER ROOM, THE EXCEPTION BEING IMMEDIATELY START MOVING TOWARDS THE NEXT ROOM AND OUT OF THE HALL.

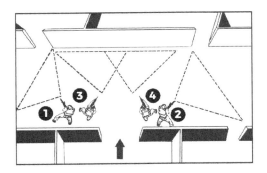
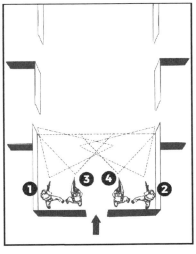

HALLWAYS

Hallways are dangerous due to the fact that bullets will travel down them and there is no form of cover. As SOP we will limit our direct movement down a hallway, moving from room to room. Entry is made in a hallway in the same method as a room. This is different from most tactics but keeps our tactics simple without compromising security. We will clear as much of the hallway from the outside and gain a foothold in the hallway by the number one man and number two man traveling down their respective walls five feet. This distance allows a foothold large enough for four personnel to enter. Once the foothold is gained, cell members can either move on-line across the hallway or in a box formation moving down a hallway.

MOUNTED OPERATIONS

DUTIES AND RESPONSIBILITIES

CONVOY LEADER: Responsible for overall conduct of convoy. Conducts brief and after-action review (AAR). Serves as navigator and lead Vehicle Commander. Responsible for equipping, organizing, and supervising preparation of assigned vehicle. Responsible for accountability of men, weapons, and equipment of assigned vehicle.

VEHICLE COMMANDER: Serves as alternate navigator. Takes direction from Convoy Leader. Responsible for equipping, organizing, and supervising preparation of assigned vehicle. Responsible for accountability of men, weapons, and equipment of assigned vehicle.

DRIVER: Operates vehicle, responsible for maintaining visual on following vehicle. Takes direction from Vehicle Commander. Responsible for PMCS, fueling, and maintaining vehicle.

SECURITY: Responsible for vehicle security. Minimum of one per vehicle. Counter assault should have multiple.

CONVOY TRACKER: Responsible for tracking convoy from base camp. Participates in convoy planning and briefs.

MOUNTED VEHICLE POSITIONS

ADVANCE: When vehicles and forces are available, use a vehicle to scout ahead of the main body to verify route and identify hazards.

LEAD: First vehicle in main body. When an advance is not available, this vehicle moves ahead, but within eyesight of the main body. Responsible for navigation and accountability. Convoy leader rides in this vehicle.

PASSENGER/CARGO: Vehicles centered in the convoy and protected by the lead and follow.

FOLLOW: Last vehicle in main body. Provides rear security, medical support, and is prepared to recover vehicles. In absence of counter assault vehicle, provide support by fire and a maneuver element.

COUNTER ASSAULT: Travels at distance behind main body. Provides a maneuver element to act as quick reaction force.

VEHICLE FORMATIONS

- Speed is security, drive as fast as safely possible

- Control convoy speeds to prevent spreading out or rear vehicle from falling behind.

- Convoy speed is determined by the slowest vehicle or the rear vehicle's ability to catch up.

- 360-degree security is necessary to prevent vehicles from approaching from any direction.

- Maintain an aggressive posture in order to keep vehicles from approaching too close.

- Vehicles One is the foundation of the formation

VEHICLE FILE

Use the Vehicle File when contact is not likely and at speed on roads. The TC will dictate the interval. Tighter intervals ensure convoy integrity in urban areas, not allowing local vehicles to penetrate our formation while larger intervals limit damage to the convoy during mechanical ambushes. Notice in above figure that vehicles are slightly staggered allowing drivers to simultaneously get a long look at the road ahead and view the following vehicle in the driver side rear view mirror. The driver side of the convoy is considered the weak side while the passenger side is considered the strong side.

TRAVELING OVERWATCH FILE

Use the Traveling Overwatch File when enemy contact is possible but not probable. The driver of the second vehicle increases his interval from the lead vehicle. This action allows the Group to use the rule of making contact with the smallest element possible, allowing the remainder of vehicle the Group to fire and support the vehicle. This formation will be used in channelized or restrictive terrain. This formation will be used when approaching illegal checkpoints, bridges, and any other time dictated by the TC. Interval will be dictated by TC.

BOUNDING OVERWATCH

Use Bounding Overwatch when enemy contact is probable but the area cannot be detoured. The driver of the first sets up in a static position that can overwatch and support with fire as the next vehicle advances to a static position that can overwatch and support with fire and the first vehicle drives past.

VEHICLE LOAD PLAN

STANDARDS: The vehicle load plan outlines the personnel and equipment needed to conduct a mounted operation. This section will cover the equipment portion of the load plan. Equipment needed for navigation, vehicle repair/recovery and contingencies will be checked at a minimum before and after operation in addition to a weekly check. Vehicle medical bag, communications equipment, and blow out bags will be loaded and checked for 100% accountability.

Conduct rehearsals to ensure equipment is serviceable and sufficient. Practice changing tires and vehicle recovery techniques once a month. This will increase proficiency and identify any additional equipment requirements.

Hydraulic floor jacks are often preferred over bottle jacks. Farm Jacks can serve several purposes, a jack, a winch, and even a spreader. Jack points are harder to find in newer vehicles. Jack types can be mixed within a vehicle convoy.

VEHICLE CHECKLIST

CONTENGENCIES/SECURITY

- ❏ VEHICLE MEDICAL BAG
- ❏ RATIONS
- ❏ WATER
- ❏ COMMUNICATIONS

- ❏ DOUBLE BASIC LOAD
- ❏ SUNDRY PACK
- ❏ 72 HOUR BAG
- ❏ SIGNAL KIT

PMCS

- ❏ PMCS COMPLETED
- ❏ FUEL

- ❏ WINDOWS/MIRRORS WASHED

NAVIGATION

- ❏ MAPS
- ❏ COMPASS

- ❏ GPS

VEHICLE REPAIR/RECOVERY

- ❏ JUMPER CABLES
- ❏ 2 QTS MOTOR OIL
- ❏ 1 GALLON COOLANT
- ❏ TIRE PRESSURE GUAGE
- ❏ WASHER FLUID
- ❏ TIRE REPAIR KIT
- ❏ TIRE INFLATOR/SEALANT
- ❏ LED FLARES

- ❏ JACK AND LUG WRENCH
- ❏ MECHANICS TOOLSET
- ❏ SIPHON HOSE
- ❏ FUSES
- ❏ LIGHT BULBS
- ❏ BELTS
- ❏ TOW STRAP
- ❏ WINDOW CLEANER

PERSONNEL RESPONSIBLE FOR CHECKS

_____

VEHICLE PMCS

Preventive Maintenance Checks and Services (PMCS) is the routine of ensuring equipment is service ready at all times. Different types of vehicles have different maintenance requirements. It is important that these requirements are located with the vehicle and followed.

The intervals of checks and services should be performed at a minimum before and after operation in addition to a weekly check.

Additional equipment and supplies required for operations should also be listed and checked at a minimum before and after operations in addition to the same weekly check.

Vehicles quickly fill up with equipment and items not tied down can become missiles during an accident. Ensure all items are secured.

Do not neglect cleaning windshields and side mirrors. Keep glass cleaner and paper towels in each vehicle and clean all before movement.

PMCS CHECKLIST

LUBRICATION
- ❏ Engine Oil Level (level, color)
- ❏ Air Filter
- ❏ Transmission Fluid (level, color, odor)
- ❏ Visually Inspect Transmission Fluid Pan for Damage / Leaks

TIRES (spare included)
- ❏ Tire Condition
- ❏ Air Pressure
- ❏ Tread Depth / Condition
- ❏ Tire Changing Equipment Present and Accessible

BRAKES
- ❏ Visually Inspect Brake System
- ❏ Brake Fluid Level/Condition
- ❏ Emergency Brake Functions

COOLING SYSTEM
- ❏ Level/Condition
- ❏ Radiator Cap
- ❏ Visually Inspect Hoses/Clamps/Thermostat for Leaks/Damage

DRIVE BELTS
- ❏ Fan and Accessory Belts
- ❏ Belt Tension/Adjustment (Approximately 1-inch movement)

BATTERY
- ❏ Visually Inspect Condition
- ❏ Visually Inspect Connections/Cables

STEERING / SUSPENSION / DRIVETRAIN
- ❏ Visually Inspect components
- ❏ Power Steering Fluid

EXHAUST SYSTEM
- ❏ Visually Inspect

LIGHTING/HORN
- ❏ Turn Signals, Lights, Horn

WINDSHIELD
- ❏ Washer Level/Operation
- ❏ Wiper Blades
- ❏ Visually Inspect Glass (Clean / No Damage)

PERSONNEL RESPONSIBLE FOR CHECKS

MOUNTED BRIEF

STANDARDS: Before every mounted operation a brief will be issued to both the participants and any individuals left behind. The parts of the brief will include the purpose of the trip, the task organization of the vehicles, routes, timeline, situation, medical, communications, and contingencies. The convoy leader is in charge of the brief and will utilize a map and graphic depicting individual positions within the convoy.

PRO TIP: Movement can become routine and though not correct; briefs are sometimes abbreviated. Always brief the full contingency plan. The time you don't brief contingencies is the time you will need it.

MOUNTED BRIEF FORMAT

1. SITUATION: Enemy and friendly situation, environmental, weather, and light data.
2. MISSION (WHO, WHAT, WHEN, WHERE, WHY)
3. TASK ORGANIZATION
                Vehicle Order of Movement
                Vehicle Task Organization
                Personnel Duties and Responsibilities
4. Timeline
                Pre Mission
                Mission Timeline
                Vehicle Refit (immediately upon return)
                After Action Review (30 minutes after return)
5. ROUTES
                Primary/Alternate
                Checkpoints
                Rally Points
6. SUPPORT
                Communications
                Medical
8. CONTENGIENCIES
                Break in Contact
                Vehicle Repair/Recovery
                Blocked Route
                Contact
9. TIME HACK

MOUNTED CONTENGENCIES

- **STANDARDS:** For mounted operations, vehicle specific contingencies are briefed before every move.

- **BREAK IN CONTACT**: If vehicles become separated, all vehicles will move to the last specified rally point. Once at rally point, security will be established. Once link up has been conducted, make decision to continue movement or return to base

- **VEHICLE REPAIR/RECOVERY**: In cases of a flat tire or disabled vehicle, security will be positioned around the vehicle. The convoy commander will move to the disabled vehicle and coordinate the repair/recovery.

- **BLOCKED ROUTE:** Move out of small arms range of the obstacle. Emplace security, bypass the route if possible. If bypass not possible, determine if obstacle can be deliberately cleared. Make decision to continue movement or return to base.

- **REACT TO CONTACT:** Identify and report location of contact.

"CONTACT RIGHT/LEFT/FRONT!"

If not in the kill zone, do not enter. Move out of small arms range, emplace security and bypass area if possible.

If in the kill zone, return fire and drive through kill zone. Consolidate outside small arms range on the far side of kill zone and position security.

Cross load ammo, evaluate any casualties and damaged vehicles. Make decision to continue mission or return to base.

If vehicles are separated by the kill zone, attempt to bypass and move to last specified rally point.

If vehicles are trapped in the kill zone, establish a support by fire position and attempt to flank the enemy element.

COMMUNICATIONS

PACE PLANNING

Life doesn't always go according to plan. That is why you need options. Thankfully, we can borrow the following planning technique. Enter the PACE Plan. **PACE** is an acronym that stands for primary, alternate, contingency and emergency. It is a methodology employed by the Green Beret to build a solid communication plan with multiple options to revert to when good turns to bad, and bad goes to worse, and worse gets to worst.

[P] Primary: The most common and most effective method of communication.

[A] Alternate: The alternative means of communicating a message if the primary fails.

[C] Contingency: This is next form of communicating if the previous fails.

[E] Emergency: The last-ditch method used when all else fails. Can be non-electronic.

PACE PLANNING ISN'T JUST FOR COMMUNICATIONS. THIS TECHNIQUE SHOULD BE USED IN ALL ASPECTS OF PLANNING.

COMMUNICATIONS PACE PLAN

PRIMARY: CELL PHONE
    P: VOICE
    A: TEXT | SHORT MESSAGE SERVICE
    C: TEXT | WIFI MESSAGING APP

ALTERNATE: RADIO
    SHORT RANGE
        P: MURS CHANNEL 3 | 151.940 FM
        A: CB CHANNEL 3 | 26.985 AM

    LONG RANGE: HAM RADIO
        HAM20M | 014.2420 USB
        HAM40M | 007.2420 LSB
        HAM60M | 005.3570 USB
        HAM80M | 003.8180 LSB

CONTINGENCY: VISUAL DISTRESS SIGNALS
    P: RED FLARE
    A: SMOKE

EMERGENCY: PHYSICAL MARKINGS

PRIMARY: CELL PHONES

The smart phone has become into a great tool in the last decade. Anything a computer can do; the smart phone can do.

When it comes to communication, the power of the cell phone is unrivaled. It is small, powerful, and can download applications tailored to your needs.

There is nothing like a good **voice call**, but there are times when a voice call will not function there is a case of damaged infrastructure (as happened during Hurricane Katrina) or calls not getting through due to overloaded circuits.

And that's when **text messages** come in handy.

Texting does not require as much bandwidth when compacted to voice calls. More often than not, when that "all circuits are busy" recording comes on, you can still count on the Short Messaging Service to relay as they run on a parallel network to cell phones.

And then there are the **data services** which could come in several shapes.

First, there is **email**. With email servers scattered all over the globe, discount email service during emergency situations at your own peril. It is highly unlikely that all servers will be down at once, so there is a fair chance it can bail you out.

There is also **social media**, with dozens of social networks accessible to you from the palm of your hand. As with email, the hosting of social media service happens on a network of global servers thus offers the added bonus of great fault tolerance and redundancy.

There are a host of **survival apps** that could be life-saving in times of disaster, from the popular ones like Google Earth and Knots 3D, to the less commonly used such as the ViewRanger GPS, Scanner Radio, Radioactivity Counter and more.

Instances of cell phone networks becoming unavailable are well known in times of disaster.

Incorporate Wi-Fi in your plan. Many times, Wi-Fi networks run on separate networks from the cell networks, meaning when cellular crashes, Wi-Fi could still be up and running.

ALTERNATE: SHORT RANGE MURS RADIO

MURS, short for Multi-Use Radio Service, are small, sturdy radio transmitters that serve as a great backup option to cell phones, although this work best in a short distance range of between two to eight miles based on terrain and obstruction, but their base stations are capable of reaching up to 20 miles.

In times of crisis, MURS is a reliable and effective communication method that will not break the bank. MURS is license-free, which means anyone can use one without the need to obtain a license from the FCC. Since the year 2000, the FCC has earmarked five MURS frequencies for public use.

These frequencies are as below:

- 151.820 MHz

- 151.880 MHz

- 151.940 MHz

- 154.570 MHz

- 154.600 MHz

But wait, with frequencies so few, won't the whole world eavesdrop on your communication?

Well, not exactly.

Each of the five MURS frequencies boasts 38 PL codes (Private Line codes), which means you have a total of 190 channels to choose from. Anyone not operating within the same PL code as you cannot hear your conversation.

These high-end walkie-talkies allow up to 2 watts of RF (radio frequency) power, which puts their communication range up to 50 times greater than unlicensed technology such as spread-spectrum and Wi-Fi.

But something else makes MURS radios different from anything else out there: the ability to get perimeter "sensors" to match your radio. They can serve as driveway alarms whereby they alert you via verbal cues when they sense any movement around your property or surrounds – thanks to IR sensors mounted around your vicinity. In terms of drawbacks, their main limitations revolve around power and range, and as with cell phones, they too can get overloaded pretty quickly when everyone is looking to use the channels. And this is where the next alternate enters…

ALTERNATE: LONG RANGE HF RADIO

The keystone to any group's communications plan is the long-range, high frequency radio communication

The Ham is not prone to range issues as its short-range counterpart. Your average five-watt handset can broadcast at least 10 miles of range on flat ground. When coupled with directional antennas and amplifiers, – it can reach halfway across the country.

HAM radio is the best communication system for virtually any kind of emergency. This is what everyone from MARS (the Military Auxiliary Radio System) and ARES (Amateur Radio Emergency Service), to the multiple emergency, search and rescue teams out there use as their emergency response system.

Unlike the MURS radio, operating a Ham radio requires a license, although getting one is not hard. Licenses are available in three main levels: Technician, General and Extra, and the higher you go, the more frequencies you can use. For starters, the lower license will have you covered, but if you need to base your communication around the world, you need to fetch the higher licenses.

Ham radios can utilize more than just voice communication. In addition to voice and Morse Code, they also use packet radio which allows for the transmission of small messages.

HAM RADIO 3-3-3 RADIO PLAN

Ham radios have frequencies instead of channel numbers, and the 3-3-3 channel for most is 146.520 MHz FM Simplex (No PL), but some prepper ham groups employ the 146.420 FM Simplex.

The 146.550 Simplex, on the other hand, is the preferred Bug Out Channel (BOC) for non-aligned survivalist hams, as well as the go-to channel

As SOP, the group will have one HAM radio and one licensed HAM Radio Operator.

CONTINGENCY: VISUAL DISTRESS SIGNALS

Throughout history, man has used visual modes of communication; light, smoke and fire. The most common visual distress signals include pyrotechnic (those that make use of flame) and non-pyrotechnic devices that you can use. Smoke signals are handy during daytime, and flares can be used both day and night. Strobes are highly visible at night.

If separated from the group, these visual distress signals are great tools that allow you to transmit your position. Use these with caution as it will also disclose your position to other individuals in the area.

When it comes to water vessels, the unspoken rule often goes that a mariner should come to the aid of a counterpart if a visual distress signal is seen. If you cannot take action yourself, you are advised to alert the nearest Coast Guard station or relevant state authority by radio. There are two channels earmarked as distress channels in the sea: Channel 9 on CB and Channel 16 on VHF marine radio (156.8 MHz).

EMERGENCY: PHYSICAL SIGNS

When all else fails, one last method you can use during times of emergency is physical signs.

Physical signs known as "hobo signals" were used by homeless travelers from the late 1800s through the Great Depression. Some rode the rails and roamed the countryside in search of work wherever they could find it, and never spending too long in any one place.

Hobos would take odd jobs than many were not willing to do. This endeared them to some, but largely, they were not tolerated. It was tough being a hobo; a life laden with challenges and danger.

It was only logical for them then to find ways to make life easier, and this led them to develop a secret language – the hobo code; a language that would lead them to food, water or work – or away from any sort of imminent danger.

Hobo signals were generally a set of symbols only they were privy to. Given most of these wanderers were illiterate, the signs had to be easy to read, but also had to look more than random markings to everyone else in order to remain cryptic. They ranged from the simple to the more cryptic.

These pictographs were scrawled in coal or chalk onto utility poles, near rail yards or other spots hobos were likely to pass. They employ this code to communicate important information about water quality, law enforcement, aggressive canines, locations that are safe to camp.

When all communication methods are down, pictographs depicting things like unsafe areas, water, shelter, security and the ability to provide a trail could prove useful.

PHYSICAL SIGNAL LIST

DANGER: **X X X**

HELP: **I I I**

MEN WITH GUNS: ←——————→

DON'T GO THIS WAY: **X**

GO THIS WAY: ⬭ ●

GO THIS WAY (PACES): (15) ●

IVE GONE HOME: ⊙

WATER: ∧∧∧

FOOD: ▭

SHELTER: ⌂

COMMUNICATIONS WINDOWS

It's not enough to know how to communicate, we need to know when to communicate and when to listen.

A good example is the 3-3-3 Radio Plan, a communication plan designed specifically for SHTF situations and can be used by anyone with a two-way radio. Often called a SKED or Radio Schedule, it is based on the "Survival Rule of Three" which basically tries to answer the "When Where and How" to establish radio contact with others.

It works like this. You turn on your radio every three hours with midnight as a starting point. Tune to Channel three every three hours and listen for at least Three minutes.

The three-hour intervals should fall at the top of the hour, every three hours:

Midnight, 3am, 6am, 9am.

Noon, 3pm, 6pm, 9pm.

Synchronize your watch with the other radio operators. You can also tune in to a radio station that broadcasts in the AM frequency as they are sure to identify their call letters every top of the hour.

You are not restricted to just the three minutes – that is recommended partly for operators to conserve battery power. If you have not connected for a while, you can hang on for about 15 minutes.

ADDITIONAL COMMUNICATION RESOURCES

GPS after SHTF

The world continues to rely more and more on GPS. What would happen to GPS satellites during TEOTWAWKI? Would they still be operational, and for how long?

Every time a GPS satellite passes within the range of a ground monitoring station, a check is completed which includes precise satellite location in space as well as their operational health. If needed, position updates are given. If by any chance the ground stations go off line, it is only a matter of time before the satellites become worthless. Modern GPS satellite has a lifespan of between 10-12 years, and even then, these satellites are dependent on constant updates without which their orbit and accuracy drifts.

Mark known points and their grids in your area so you can determine when accuracy has been compromised.

This is why as a survivalist, you need to be all-rounded and learn how to navigate the traditional way using a compass and map, and probably a sextant and sight-reduction tables.

Beacons

A tracking system in a SHTF situation might prove to be invaluable. Given the circumstances, however, we know a cell-based or GPS-based system would be hard to count on. Well, the latter could work but its signal could be affected in such cases as dense wooded areas.

A great option for a tracking device would be the Marco Polo Advanced Tracking System for pets (it can be multi-purpose) because it uses neither GPS, nor cell service. One of the lightest and tiniest RC model tracking and recovery solutions on the market today, it operates more like a homing beacon.

This unique tracking device has a range of up to two miles (which is impressive), with a transmitter battery that can last up to 45 days while being monitored continuously.

SEARCH AND ASSESMENT MARKINGS

It is important to understand the symbols used by Federal and State agencies. These markings usually follow the FEMA SEARCH ASSESNENT MARKING SYSTEM.

A spray painted "X" is left near the main entrance of the building. In the left portion of the "X", the team conducting the search is input. In the top portion of the "X" the date and time of the start of the search is input.

The number of live victims removed is written in the bottom of the "X". The number of dead victims found would also be written. Persons unaccounted for and/or location of other victims is written below the square.

Additional information on hazards pertaining to the structure is written in the right portion of the "X".

Reference to building floor numbers would use the ground as G, 1 as the first floor above G. B1 as the first floor below G, and so forth. This is contrasted with US floor numbering that starts with 1 as the ground level. "DOA" would stand for "dead on arrival". "LB" would stand for "live bodies". "DB" would stand for "dead bodies found". "0-0" would stand for "no bodies, no survivors found".

FEMA SEARCH ASSESSMENT MARKING

PA-TF-1 18 SEP 00 1800	• SINGLE SLASH UPON ENTRY INTO STRUCTURE • TF ID, DATE & ENTRY TIME NOTED • INDICATES ONGOING SEARCH
18 SEP 00 2130 PA-TF-1 18 SEP 00 1800	• CROSSING SLASH UPON EXIT • UPON EXIT, DATE AND TIME NOTED IN TOP FIELD • ADDITIONAL INFORMATION PLACED IN OPEN AREAS OF "X"
18 SEP 00 2130 PA-TF-1 18 SEP 00 1800 RATS 8 L 3 D	• RIGHT- HAZARDS • BOTTOM- # OF VICTIMS

MEDICAL

INDIVIDUAL FIRST AID KIT

An Individual First Aid Kit (IFAK) is required for every individual in the group. It can be carried in your vehicle, on your person, or in your blow out bag. Just make sure your IFAK is in a location that is easy to access and members know of its location. It is preferable to have this in a fanny pack. If wearing, the five or eight o clock position on the body is ideal for placement. This insures that it is out of the way of anything on your pistol belt and you can still rapidly draw your side-arm without any issues. Insure that you can get to your pistol magazines and rifle mag (if you have one) on your gun belt without any issue. Do what works for you, but make sure that you are able to get the contents out yourself should the need arise. Remember that your IFAK is for your personal use only. If treating a fellow group member, treat that member with their own IFAK. Try to never use your IFAK for anyone else. Additional unused tourniquets can be placed in your gear and vehicle within easy reach of both hands. Additional tourniquets and small pressure dressings can be carried in my cargo pockets along with a chest seal.

IFAK CONTENTS

- 1X S.O.F.T. TOURNIQUET

- 2X CHEST SEALS

- 2X 10 OR 14 GAUGE NEEDLES

- 1X HEMOSTATIC GAUZE

- 1X EMERGENCY TRAUMA BANDAGE

- 1X CASUALTY CARD

- 1X 3 INCH WHITE TAPE

- 1X SHARPIE

- 1X NPA (28 FRANK)

- 1X PETROLUEM JELLY (FOR NPA)

- 1X SMALL CRIC KIT

- 2X GLOVES (YOUR SIZE)

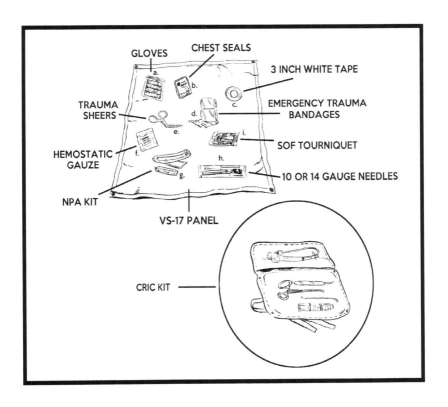

GLOVES
CHEST SEALS
3 INCH WHITE TAPE
a.
b.
c.
TRAUMA SHEERS
d.
EMERGENCY TRAUMA BANDAGES
e.
i.
SOF TOURNIQUET
HEMOSTATIC GAUZE
f.
h.
10 OR 14 GAUGE NEEDLES
g.
NPA KIT
VS-17 PANEL
CRIC KIT

SMARCH

S.) SECURITY

- As with everything, security is the first priority. You are unable to help a casualty of you yourself becomes a casualty.

- Direct casualty if possible to provide self-aid and move to your location.

- Move casualty out of immediate area to secure location.

- If situation and time permit, apply the tourniquet proximal to the bleeding site as high on the extremity as possible, over the uniform, tighten, and move the casualty to cover.

M.) MASSIVE HEMORRHAGING

- Once in a safe location, reassess any previously applied tourniquets.

- Stop massive hemorrhaging first by exposing wound and applying tourniquet or tourniquet like device proximal to wound site. For pelvic wounds pack with gauze and use a combat clamp, or improvise with a Nalgene bottle or similar device over the wound and wrap tightly. If the wound is located on an extremity, apply as high on the limb as possible and tighten down until bleeding stops.

- Reassess all interventions frequently

A.) AIRWAY

- Casualties with an altered level of consciousness should be disarmed immediately

- For unconscious patients without an airway obstruction, perform a chin lift or jaw thrust maneuver. If casualty permits, put a lubricated nasopharyngeal airway into the right nostril first with beveled end facing the center of the nose and tape it down. If right nostril is unsuccessful, try in left nostril. Rotate lubricated nasopharyngeal airway 180 degrees with beveled end facing center of nose and go in halfway then rotate 180 degrees until it stops.

- If unconscious, put casualty in recovery position.

- If conscious follow same steps as above and allow casualty to assume any position that best protects his/her airway to include sitting up.

- If casualty has difficulty breathing, has maxillofacial trauma, or has severe burns especially around the face, perform a cricothyroidotomy. Locate the cricothyroid membrane below the Adams apple. In most humans, it is one finger down from the Adams apple. It will feel soft in comparison to the surrounding area and indent when a finger runs across it. Make a 2-inch vertical incision with a scalpel (preferably) or a knife. Once the membrane is exposed, rotate your blade and horizontally incise the membrane. Input endotracheal tube through the membrane and into the trachea. Inflate the bulb with 10cc of air. Observe misting in the tube caused by perspiration from inhalation and exhalation if the casualty's breathing. If possible, put a bag valve mask over the connecting portion of the endotracheal tube and squeeze the bag every time you breathe. Check proper placement, if possible, by a stethoscope placed on the chest listening simultaneously for breath sounds as someone bags. If no stethoscope is available, use your ears.

R.) RESPIRATIONS

- Expose the casualty's chest and look for any wounds, including under the armpits, or serious bruising. If penetrating chest wounds are found, clean the wound first, then apply an occlusive dressing. If unavailable, duct tape over the wound. Put your ear to the dressing and listen to insure it is sealed properly. If not sealed properly, apply another occlusive dressing or like material and reassess.

- Check causality's back for entry/exit wounds. If penetrating wounds are found, apply occlusive dressings and assess them to ensure a good seal has been made.

- In all casualties with progressive respiratory distress and known or suspected torso trauma, consider a tension pneumothorax and decompress the chest on the side of the injury with a 14-gauge, 3.25-inch needle/catheter unit inserted in the second intercostal space at the midclavicular line. For rapid placement, put your hand underneath casualty's armpit and press your thumb naturally towards his/her upper chest. This is anatomically an acceptable location for the needle decompression. Remember to insert the needle and then go up and over the rib rather than down when applying. Going beneath the rib increases the probability of cutting the underlying nerves, arteries, and vein bundles that run below ribs.

C.) CIRCULATION

- Assess for unrecognized hemorrhages and control all sources of bleeding. Reassess all previous tourniquets. For wounds not located in the chest or stomach, pack them with combat gauze until the wound cavity is completely full. Then apply a pressure bandage over the wound applying more circumferential pressure with each wrap. Secure the pressure dressing on itself.

- When time and tactical situation permit, check the distal pulse of any extremity that has a tourniquet. If a pulse is still felt, retighten the correlating tourniquet.

H.) HEAT, I.V.'S, EYE INJURIES, AND OTHER INTERVENTIONS

- Apply blankets to casualty to keep him/her warm.

- If Pt. can swallow, have him/her take a combat pill pack (moxifloxacin/avelox 400mg orally, Mobic 15 mg, Tylenol 650mg) DO NOT USE NSAIDS (Naproxen, Ibuprofen. They inhibit your ability to make platelets that are needed for clotting wounds).

- Start 18 gauge I.V. in an extremity that doesn't have an injury. Run it very slow until medic can assess casualty.

- For penetrating eye injuries, if situation permits, perform an immediate visual acuity test. Have the casualty follow your finger in a square then figure 8 pattern. Cover the eye with a rigid shield (not a pressure patch). Once to a secure location, cover both eyes.

- Splint any fractures in a position that looks natural. Check for pulses in the broken limb before and after splinting. If no pulse is found inform medic.

- Reassess all interventions.

- Document everything you've done on a casualty card or paper.

MEDICAL SHED SOP

Set up a primary and alternate medical room. If you can find a hardened structure to place your med shed in, it is preferred. You don't want the place where you bring wounded people to be easily destroyed. The primary med shed consists of at least two hard litters set on sawhorses or litter stands. Each of the handles are used to hold items immediately needed when treating a casualty.

Put two of the new C.A.T tourniquets on one handle. On the other handle, put a new BVM hooked to a full oxygen tank that is kept underneath the litter. Put a stethoscope and a pulse ox on one of the handles as well. Use a hypothermia blanket to drape on top of the litter; open it up, roll it up, and stow the rest underneath itself where the Pt's feet go. A heated blanket should be stored at the feet. This creates a good blood barrier that makes it very easy to keep your litter and room clean. It also insures you have a ready, high quality space blanket and heated blanket to apply to your Pt fast.

Along the wall above the litter, put a rapid I.V kit that consists of 500ml Hextend, I.V. Line, 10ml vial of TXA with a 100ml bag wrapped with its own I.V. Line. Tape two Aveolox pills, two vials of Rocephin, and two vials of Ancef. I also tape two 14, 16, and 18 gauge catheters on the wall beside the bag. Beside the I.V. Set I tape a cric and intubation kit to the wall in its package ready to go as well. Each bed has a standalone trauma sheet within arm's reach of the middle of the bed.

Pack the trauma kit from top to bottom/ left to right based on tier level of what I would need to grab. The top left of the trauma sheet consists of tourniquets, to the right of that is hemostatic gauze (celox is preferred due to its ability to work on anyone even old contractors with strange blood disorders unlike quick clot). Underneath that to the left are pressure dressings, to the right of that pouch are chest seals/ decompression needles. The rest of the sheet is cric kits, burn kits, splinting material, and I.V. supplies.

There is a large burn kit along the wall in the center of the two beds. In the primary med room, place all sick call/ trauma meds as well. Ensure there is additional shelving along the wall. Consider using drilled screws and wrapped 550 cord on the outside of the shelving to create a railing to insure meds do not fall off. Divided the shelving into sections such as antibiotics, antihistamines, cardiac drugs, etc. This makes it very easy to secure all of your important meds and primary med shed in one. Around the room hang and tape 30-minute high intensity yellow chemical lights to be used as a lighting source if the power is out. As soon as you walk in the door to the left in the primary room we kept large red chemical-lights. It is S.O.P that if someone brings a Pt into the room, a red chemical-light is cracked and thrown outside the door letting everyone on the camp know there was a casualty in there.

The alternate medical room is set up just like the primary room except it is one bed instead of two. If your Primary room is smaller, the alternate also enables the group to have adequate room to triage casualties needed. Keep a few of the pelican cases ready accessible and stocked with trauma supplies. These can be positioned out of the way along the wall. Always chose a room and area that is easy to maneuver in and out with a litter. The middle of the floor is always kept clear. If you have the supplies, put a ventilator, suction machine, and vital signs monitor close to all of the beds. Place at least one dry erase board per room and write Pt. Name, age, method of injury (MOI), treatments; times, etc., with spaces to fill in the blanks.

TRAUMA SHEETS

TRAUMA SHEET

Work top to bottom left to right in tier level of what is needed first in a severe casualty

A. First Pouch 10X Tourniquets

B. Second Pouch 10X Gauze

C. Third Pouch 5X ETD and 5XETD Abdominal

D. Fourth Pouch 10X Chest Seals 10 Times 14 Gauge Needle Decompression needles

E. Fifth Pouch X5 Sam Splints X10 Cravats

F. Sixth Pouch X10 burn dressings.

G. Bottom Pouch X3 LR 500ml Bags X3 NS 500Ml Bags X10 18 gauge needles X10 15 or 10 GTT drip sets X

H. 20 alcohol pads X20 iodine pads

PRIMARY MED SHED PACKING LIST

- 1X package of red chemical-lights for primary CCP

- 2X Litter Stands

- 2X Talon Litters

- 2X O2 tanks2X Times BVM

- 2X Pulse OX

- 2X Stethoscope

- 2X Heated Blanket and Space Blanket

- 2X 500ml Hextend or Hetastarch

- 2X 10Gtt or 15Gtt Set

- 2X 14,16,18,20-gauge catheter

- 2X Suction 90-=

- 2X Vital Signs Monitor

- 2X Ventilator

- 2X Constricting Band

- 2X Trauma Sheers

- 6X SOF-T Tourniquets

- 2X Rocephin

- 2X Ancef

- 2X 100ml bag with 1 gram TXA

- 2X aveolox

- 1X large burn blanket

- 2X cric and intubation kit

- 2X Chest tube kit

- 2X Trauma Sheets Packed as per S.O.P

- All sick call drugs placed either on the wall with organic shelving or in a place where they can be organized and categorized neatly.

- Alternate Med Shed has everything primary med shed has just X1 instead of X2. Place all team organic delta boxes in alternate med shed opened and accessible. Keep middle of rooms open and free.

- Alternate med shed has 1 box of large yellow chemical lights.

- 10X high intensity chemical lights in case power goes out (put within arm's reach at strategic locations to illuminate whole room)

MASS CASUALTY PROCEDURES

A mass casualty incident or MASCAL is defined by any event that overwhelms immediately available medical capabilities to include personnel, supplies, and or equipment. In layman's terms, a mass Cal can consist of two casualties and only one I.F.A.K, or a medic, fully stocked aid bag, and 5 casualties. Both circumstances overwhelm the medical personnel. First secure an area such as a building or room to funnel patients in so triage can be conducted. Once this has been established cordon the area and maintain constant security on the entries and exits. Extra personnel should be inside the room to pass up information to higher and help with first aid of all casualties. Place two people at a funnel point outside of the room. One of them preferably needs to be a medic or nurse. These two people can begin by shouting loudly for any injured personnel to move towards them. Security should be vigilant and check incoming personnel. At the funnel point the medic will examine and triage the casualty based upon their injuries.

TRIAGE CATEGORIES

Minimal (Green) ambulatory casualties: "Walking Wounded" (no impaired function, can self-treat or be cared for non-professionally) abrasions, contusions, minor lacerations etc. Minimal (green) personnel if capable can provide first aid treatments or be used as support for expectant personnel.

Delayed (Yellow) Wounded casualties: in need of surgery but whose general condition permits delay without endangering life, limb, or eyesight. Can include blunt or penetrating torso injuries without signs of shock, fractures, soft-tissue injuries without significant bleeding, facial fractures without airway compromise, or survivable burns without immediate threat to life.

Red (Immediate) Critical casualties: seriously injured, but have a reasonable chance of survival. Requires immediate attention within minutes to 2 hours on arrival to avoid death or major disability. Can include airway obstruction, tension pneumothorax, uncontrolled hemorrhage, amputations, head injury that needs decompression, torso, neck, or pelvic injuries with shock.

Black (Expectant) Casualties: show obvious signs of death. This group has injuries that overwhelm current medical resources at the expense of treating salvageable patients. These casualties should never be abandoned but separated from view of the other casualties. They should be given comfort and attention. No one should have to die alone. Black should include unresponsive with no pulse, catastrophic head injuries/ chest injuries, burns without reasonable chance for survival, or high spinal cord injuries. Expectant personnel should be separated from all other categories and someone on the group should stay with the casualty. Maintain rapport and provide as much comfort as possible.

Once the medic at the choke point properly triages the casualty he will then place him in the appropriate spot based off of the casualty's triage category. The casualty will then be given either a chemical light or ribbon of the same color that correlates with the triage category on the casualty's arm or leg. If there are suspected casualties that cannot move on their own, security will be pushed out and personnel will go get them off the battlefield and bring them to the funnel point.

The medic at the choke point of the room is responsible for keeping track of all personnel entering and leaving the area, insuring casualties are in the correct treatment categories and being assessed, passing information to the leadership and coordinating casualties to exfil if possible. He should not be treating casualties; he should be managing everyone else who is treating casualties.

PREVENTATIVE MEDICINE

Preparing for emergency situations starts with preparing your body. Preventative medicine includes maintaining and optimizing your current physical health. You should be in good physical shape, not use any tobacco products, illicit drugs or alcohol, and eat nutritious foods- the same measures that extend life in non-emergency situations. Taking a daily multivitamin keeps your body functioning well.

If you are on medications for chronic conditions such as heart disease, high cholesterol, etc., ask your doctor for an emergency supply in case of a crisis. Maintenance medications often times can be refilled for 90 days at a time if you use a service such as Meds by Mail. While at the doctor's office, update your vaccinations, especially tetanus. If you have not been vaccinated for hepatitis, now is the time and if you have not had chicken pox or the chicken pox vaccine, add that on. Get a flu shot every year. Another important consideration is your training for medical emergencies. Basic CPR and first aid classes are inexpensive and can save lives. Additionally, dental problems can have a significant effect on general health. In crisis situations continue oral hygiene including brushing your teeth, flossing and using mouthwash.

In an emergency situation, bacteria will be a serious danger. Wounds of any size may become infected and lead to sepsis and death. All wounds should be cleaned with hydrogen peroxide and promptly covered. Stock up on simple band-aids for small wounds, butterfly bandages to close cuts, and sterile gauze and medical tape to cover and protect larger wounds. Other people will also be a source of bacteria and viruses. Prepare to reduce the spread of debilitating infectious diseases such as the flu and bronchitis by having surgical N95 masks and frequently using alcohol-based hand sanitizer. In case of close living conditions, use quarantine precautions for the infected person to protect the community.

Store plenty of baking soda, borax and vinegar. These will be basic cleaners for yourself and your home. With these three you will be amazed at just how clean you can get surfaces and people!

Consider storing various sized trash cans and tight-fitting lids. The days of the swing top cans will be gone. You will now be concerned with pests and their access to your trash both indoors and outdoors. Get rid of those open top containers and have replacements with tight fitting lids. You can store these by sinking the cans inside one another with the lids on. If the lids don't fit on zip tie them to the handles of the cans. Include plenty of trash bags for the sized cans you plan to use. Also, get your hands on plenty nitrile gloves, dust masks and even some disposable aprons. You could invest in some shoe covers as well but my recommendation would be to keep all shoes outside.

The next step is to prepare for common health situations. First and foremost, a simple case of diarrhea can kill in a crisis situation. Dehydration occurs quickly leading to unconsciousness and death. In most cases of diarrhea, the body is expelling a toxin, so do not take an anti-diarrheal. Instead, stock up on oral rehydration salts or waters with added electrolytes such as Pedialyte to replenish what is lost. Another common event is an allergic reaction to a medicine, toxin or organic material in the field. Benadryl (diphenhydramine) can be taken to calm the body's reaction and can also be used for anxiety and insomnia. Persons with known severe allergies (anaphylactic shock) should keep several Epi-pens.

Common injuries can compromise otherwise healthy individuals. To minimize downtime, keep on hand supplies for sprains and strains. This includes compression bandages small enough for ankles and larger ones for knees or shoulders, as well as ankle and knee braces and slings for injured arms and collarbones. Using compression bandages limits the body's ability to swell, keeping valuable fluids in circulation rather than concentrated around a sprain. Additionally, keep a supply of instant ice packs to limit pain and swelling, casting bandages in case of closed fractures and a pair of crutches so the injured are not immobile.

This list is intended to get you started on thinking about preparedness beyond food and water and is not inclusive and should be developed as part of the group plan. Be sure to keep you and your groups general health in mind when collecting and storing supplies. Beyond the items already listed, you should keep a stockpile of meds and supplies that will reduce the need for additional medical attention.

This includes:

- **Acetaminophen for pain and fevers**
- **Activated charcoal tablets in case of ingesting poison**
- **Alcohol based hand sanitizer**
- **Alcohol pads**
- **Arm sling**
- **Baking soda for toothpaste**

- Band-aids, Kerlix, rolled and flat gauze

- Compression (ACE) bandages

- CPR Mask

- Crutches

- Emergency dental kit with filling putty

- Hydrogen peroxide for wounds and mouthwash

- Instant cold packs

- Knee and ankle brace

- Magnifying glass

- Medical tape and paper tape in case of allergies

- Medi-Lyte electrolye tablets Suture kits

- Petroleum jelly to make gauze dressings less porous

- Sterile Nitrile Gloves

- Table salt to gargle for respiratory infections

- Tweezers

RATIONS

The planning and act of food storage in preparedness should be a top priority. The 1944 Minnesota Starvation Experiment researched the effects of starvation on the human body. The study called for the men to lose 25 percent of their normal body weight. The first three months involved a normal diet of 3,200 calories a day, followed by six months of semi-starvation at 1,570 calories a day.

The food consisted of the limited rations available in wartime Europe. The subjects worked 15 hours a day and were also forced to walk 22 miles a week. During the semi-starvation phase the changes were drastic. The test subjects had significant decreases in stamina, strength, sex drive, and heart rate.

Psychological effects included fatigue, lack of motivation, depression, and elevated irritability (Keramidas). Mental abilities also begin degrade as your brain literally uses its neurons for nourishment.

These effects put in motion a physical and physiological deficit that is increasingly hard to recover.

Simply put, once your body starts to starve, you begin to lose the abilities that you need to survive creating a vicious cycle that is hard to break.

So again, food storage and the abilities to sustain yourself should be one of your top priorities.

EATING WHAT YOU STORE

The most important part of successful food storage is storing what you like. The matter of taste is so important because you will be sustaining yourself on the various foods that you have stored. If you must use this food and have no other options chances are your family will be dealing with problems greater than just hunger.

Under such stress your family will not be sleeping well or eating right. Therefore, having foods that they enjoy on hand will make all the difference.

The best way to go about this is to ask your family about some of their favorite dinners, snacks and ingredients. To get a full spectrum of ingredients and meals tell each member of your family to write out a week of their favorite meals for breakfast, lunch and dinner. Though you may not be able to make or find these foods you can use this list when buying pre-made food storage.

Remember you can also purchase freeze dried ingredients as well. If you cannot find what you need in dried food seek it out in canned. As long as you rotate often you will be able to store a variety of ingredients that your family loves to eat.

Another very important aspect of families eating food storage is to eat some today. Don't wait until everything changes to break out the food storage. If you can integrate some of these ingredients into your weekly menus today you will not have a complete shock to the system. Use item that stand out as well. Don't just use dehydrated peas in your beef stew. Rather use Canned beef or dehydrated chicken in your entrees.

During a disaster people get unhinged as radical change is forced upon them. Make sure mealtime is a time of comfort for your family.

FOOD STORAGE OPTIONS

When it comes to long term food storage, focus on these three main categories. These three will hold the longest and require little care or oversight.

- Freeze Dried

- Dehydrated

- Canned

FREEZE DRIED FOOD

The process of freeze drying removes the moisture from food at below freezing temperatures. Without the moisture content bacteria struggle to grow and the food has a greater shelf life.

This is the best available option for food storage. The advantage to freeze dried foods is that they have an incredible shelf life when stored properly. Freeze dried foods also retain the nutrient content better than any other process. This makes them one of the best options for your long-term food storage. The disadvantage of this process is the cost. You will spend more on freeze dried foods than you will on any other type.

DEHYDRATED FOOD

The process of dehydration works in a similar manner but rather than use freezing temperatures the dehydrations process uses air flow. This removes the moisture and starves the bacteria just as the freeze-drying process does.

Dehydrated foods are cheaper than freeze dried but do to the process they do not retain as much of the nutrition. That is not to say these foods couldn't satiate you they just aren't as nutrient dense has freeze dried. Dehydrated foods will last a very long time as well. When stored properly these foods will last for up to 30 years. This makes them one of the best options for long term food storage.

CANNED FOOD

The process of canning pulls affects shelf life by pulling another crucial resource from the bacteria. The canning process removes oxygen from whatever is being canned. By doing this the bacteria are starved of precious oxygen and they either die or unable to proliferate. Canned foods do not have the shelf life that dehydrated and freeze-dried foods possess. They are still a great option for your food storage plans.

FAT STORAGE

There are several things we take for granted when creating our food storage plans. One of them is salt and pepper. It's always around and you never really think about how you would get it once it runs out. Salt is vital to our bodies performance but it's rarely part of food storage plans.

More important than salt is fat. Another essential part of the human body. Fat can be harvested from animals but I am talking about fats that you don't have to hunt for. These fats will be vital when attempting to perform any type of cooking. There are many types of fat that you can begin to store today for tough times.

The thing about fats is that they are not all created equal. Some fats are better for high heat than others. Some are better for simply flavoring. Below I will profile some of the most popular fats in the market so you can decide which of these will best suit your needs.

COCONUT OIL

If you are going to store one type of fat, prioritize coconut oil. This is an incredibly beneficial fat that helps your body in many ways. It can be used to sauté and burns at a higher temperature than olive oil. Coconut oil stores well and also doubles as a great option for skin care.

OLIVE OIL

It's an absolute powerhouse when it comes to what it can do for your body. A concentration of healthy saturated fats and great flavor as well. One of the biggest problems with olive oil is its low smoke point. This means it burns very easily at normal cooking temperatures. High heat also destroys the flavor of the oil and what you are cooking it in.

VEGETABLE OIL

Vegetable oil has been a staple in American homes for generations. It is not made from vegetables; this oil is made from seeds. Vegetable oil is a manmade oil and not really good for your body. It's very cheap and could be a solution to mix in with other oils. Do not rely on vegetable oil alone.

The last 20 years have been framed by a rush towards low fat or no fat diets. Fat is a necessary part of your body functioning properly. In men, fat is crucial to creating testosterone. Don't leave these crucial options out of your food storage program.

TIERED FOOD STORAGE

When storing food, tier your supplies for quick, intermediate, and long-term use. This method gives you more options depending on the environment we find ourselves in. These tiers can be stored in different locations for added security and redundancy.

QUICK USE: At least one month of food should be stored in a way to transport quickly and use immediately. The best example of this would be MRE's or other foodstuffs in individual ready to eat packaging. MRE's meals have come a long way. These meals are all you need in one bag and do not need to be hydrated by boiling water. One military MRE's has on average 1250 calories and 1/3 of your necessary vitamins and minerals. Individual MRE's come in boxes of 12 and have on average 15,000 total calories. Stored at 80 degrees, these boxes will last over six years. One box per week will provide one individual with over 2100 calories a day.

INTERMEDIATE USE: An additional three months of food stuffs should be stored in a way that's easy to use but not quite as easy to move or complete. An example of this would be canned foods and smaller packages of rice and noodles. These items should have the ability to be prepared in a matter of 30 minutes. These items should also be part of your daily home food stock and rotated to continually keep up to date.

LONG TERM: The subject matter experts in long term food storage are the Church of Jesus Christ and Latter-Day Saints. They encourage a culture of self-reliance including storing food and water. As such, they have a wealth of resources including the purchase of bulk food items. A long-term food supply should be one years' worth of basic foods. The following is a recommended yearly minimum for long term storage per person: **GRAINS: 400 LBS, LEGUMES: 60 LBS, POWDERED MILK: 16 LBS, COOKING OIL: 10 QUARTS, SUGAR OR HONEY: 60 LBS, SALT: 8 LBS.** These bulk supplies should be augmented with freeze dried food. Some meals are basically all you need in one bag that is completely hydrated by boiling water. Other dehydrated food come in bulk via #10 cans. Most of these meals can be prepared in a matter of 20 minutes and are a great way to add to your bulk supplies.

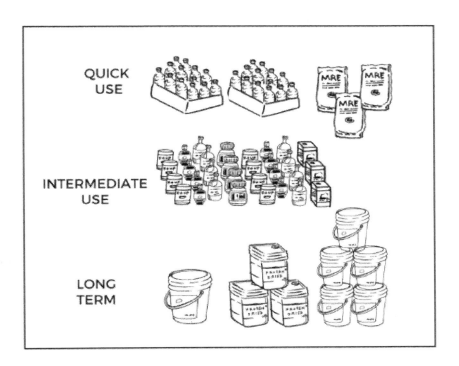

CREATING A MEAL PLAN

Long-term storage lists are generally a minimum guideline; we need a plan. Food menus should to be planned and tailored for you, your family, your group, and your region. As we previously discussed, starvation diets will not equip you to excel in a survival situation. Calories need to be factored in. Other considerations include are the foods storable, realistic, and not prohibitively expensive.

CREATING YOUR MEAL PLAN:

1. LIST 7 MAIN MEALS YOUR FAMILY WILL EAT.

2. LIST 3 BREAKFASTS YOUR FAMILY WILL EAT.

3. LIST 3 LUNCHES YOUR FAMILY WILL EAT.

4. CALCULATE CALORIES NEEDED PER DAY FOR EACH INDIVIDUAL.

5. SEARCH FOR RECIPES AND COMPILE A LIST OF INGREDIENTS AND ITS NUTRITIONAL VALUE.

6. TEST RECIPE FOR TASTE; BE SURE TO TEST MULTIPLE PREPARATION METHODS.

7. MULTIPLY INGREDIENTS BY NUMBER OF TIMES PREPARED PER YEAR.

8. STORE YOUR INGREDIENTS AND INCORPORATE RECIPE IN YOUR NORMAL MEAL PLAN.

EXAMPLE RECIPE TO BE INCORPORATED: An example of this method could be the following. I have determined that my meal plan will incorporate a high protein loaf of bread at a rate of once a week. I searched for recipes that are storable and use ingredients me and my family can eat. I used allrecipe.com and found a high protein bread recipe. Use a recipe convertor to multiply the ingredients based on your servings. For this conversion, 1 year or 53 weeks' worth.

HIGH PROTEIN LOAF INGREDIENT LIST

- 2 teaspoons active dry yeast

- 1 cup bread flour

- 1 cup whole wheat flour

- 1/4 cup soy flour

- 1/4 cup powdered soy milk

- 1/4 cup oat bran

- 1 tablespoon canola oil

- 1 tablespoon honey

- 1 teaspoon salt

- 1 cup water

HIGH PROTEIN LOAF INGREDIENT LIST (53 LOAFS)

- 2 Cups, 4 Tablespoons active dry yeast

- 28 Pounds bread flower

- 28 Pounds wheat flour

- 7.3 Pounds soy flour

- 7 Pounds powdered soy milk

- 7 Pounds oat bran

- 3 Cups, 5 Tablespoons canola oil

- 3 Cups, 5 Tablespoons honey

- 1 Cups, 1 Tablespoons, 2 Teaspoons salt

- 3.4 Gallon water

NUTRITIONAL VALUE

- Total Calories: 1370 kcal

- Total Fats: 24 g

- Total Carbs: 241g

- Total Protein: 65 g

- Total Cholesterol: 0 mg

- Total Sodium: 2350 mg

FOOD STORAGE

Now that there is a plan of what we need to store, we need to focus on how we store it. Your food storage is the food that will keep you, your family, and your group alive in the event of a serious disaster. There are some very serious considerations that need to go into the location or locations of your food storage

- Temperature

- Moisture

- Security

- Visitors

TEMPERATURE

Your food storage is only as good as the environment in which it is stored. Seals and the contents of cans or even Mylar bags are subject to freezing temperatures as well as extremes of heat. You must be very careful not to store your food in a garage or other area where the temperature fluctuates.

These variants in temperature will have adverse effects not just on the food you are storing but on the vessel in which it's being stored. The food may survive the temperature change pests could wind up infiltrating cracks and holes in the storage vessel. This means the food will not be there when you need it.

MOISTURE

Of course, when dealing with dry foods it's important that you keep the moisture away from them. This makes basements another area of contention, if you are subject to leaks. The moisture will also rust cans and produce mold. Moisture is just as much an enemy to your food storage as is the temperature.

Moisture will fuel the production of bacteria as well as the growth of mold. These things are terrifying realities of what you might be dealing with when you open that food in a post disaster. This moisture must never have access to your food and you should check your storage locations often.

KITCHEN SETUP

Establishing a kitchen is essential to individual or group survival. There are major safety and preventive medicine concerns when processing foods and doing any kind of cooking in a survival situation. By following the guidelines below and identifying an experienced individual as the group's food services chief, you can create a safe, functional kitchen setup.

SETUP LOCATION: The first consideration is the location of your camp kitchen. Set your kitchen up downwind of from the main living area and away and uphill of any latrines. You should set your cooking operation up 100 yards away from your actual camp. In this situation washing up after eating and head back to your camp is advised.

HYGIENE: Preparing food to safely eat begins with ensuring that the people who prepare the food are health and have good hygiene. The food services chief most make certain that workers wash their hands, are wearing clean clothes, and are not sick. Individuals are required to inform higher if they suspect they are sick.

HANDWASHING STATIONS: Hands should be washed with soap and water before handling anything in the kitchen area and often throughout duty. Additionally, handwashing stations should be located in the living area, outside the latrines, near the kitchen and dining area, and any other appropriate areas.

FIXED BLADE KNIFES AND CUTTING BOARDS: These are the processing pieces of the kitchen. Cutting on the board and using the knife to trip and slice. These are indispensable tools. Be sure to use a knife exclusive to the kitchen. Set these two items on a tree stump of some elevated area.

SPICES AND OILS: These are flavorings, seasonings and lubrication. If you are going to be cooking directly on a grate or on a skillet you will need some oil or fat for that to work out best. The cooking oil is also a great base for margination.

GRATES, POTS, AND PANS: This is the cooking hardware. You can put your camping pots and pans directly into the fire but that will take years off their life. The small pot is for boiling water and the larger cast iron Dutch over is a multipurpose piece of equipment. Base the size of your pots on the size of your family or group.

UTENSILS, SERVING SPOONS, AND SPATULAS: These items are all about handling food. If you are cooking raw meats or handling food you will want to have a way to handle that food. When you are cooking foods in liquid the slotted spoon is worth its weight in gold. The fish spatula is great for camping because it's nice and compact.

STOVES AND OVENS: A camp kitchen is based on cooking on the camp fire. We should be trained and prepared to cook over open fire but this is not the most effective means. A wood burning outdoor stove build from block is easy to build and more efficient. Regardless, depending on your skill level and the conditions, fire doesn't always start. Be sure you have several methods of cooking. Propane stores great and is a very efficient way to cook. A 20lb propane tank can last a small family, one meal a day, for one month. Regardless of cooking method, keep a fire extinguisher available.

WASHING PROCEDURES: It is very important to thoroughly sanitize cooking equipment. Unfortunately, this uses water which is often a valuable commodity. Mitigate this by stocking up on paper plates and plastic utensils. The procedures listed below should be used when washing pots and pans.

Scrape: Remove all food particles from dishes.

Presoak: Set up a bucket with a warm soapy solution to loosen grease and remove any food particles unable to be scraped off.

Wash: Fill a sink or second bucket with hot soapy water and wash the items. Change the soapy water as needed. Shake off as much soap as possible before the first rinse.

First Rinse: Set up a second sink or bucket with water to remove any leftover soap.

Second Rinse: This rinse is for sanitation. A water temperature to 170 degrees for 30 seconds is needed for sterilization by heat. A less resource intensive method is chemically sanitizing which bleach. Soak for at least two minutes in a solution of 2 teaspoons of bleach per 1 gallon of water.

Dry: Do not dry pots and pans with towels and napkins as this can spread bacteria. Have a rack area to air dry items.

FOOD WASTE MANAGEMENT: Food scraps, oil, and dirty water draws rodents and insects. It is critical you remove any food waste from the area immediately. Food can be buried or burned, just insure it is well away from your living and cooking area. Liquids can be disposed of in a soak pit.

BASIC CAMP KITCHEN LIST: The following is for a basic small kitchen setup and can be scaled up as needed. Look for utensils and containers that will all fit within the Dutch oven. The end state is to have your entire camping kitchen inventory contained in the Dutch oven. This will save you space in your pack for other things. If the Dutch oven has a nice carrying handle this becomes a very mobile kitchen. If not wrap it in a few lengths of towel or wrap it in paracord that can easily be removed before cooking.

Equipment

- Fixed Blade Knife

- Can Opener

- Small Cutting board

- Small container of salt and pepper mix (1/3 pepper 2/3 salt)

- Small container of cooking oil

- Small Grate

- Small lightweight pot with handle

- Cast Iron Dutch Oven with a Handle

- Solid Spoon, Slotted Spoon

- Grain Mill

- Tongs

- Utensils

- Small butane stove

- Micro camping stove for backup

- Dish Soap

- Paper Plates

WATER

If you plan to utilize dehydrated or freeze-dried foods than you must have clean water to rehydrate. These needs must be calculated into your already affirmed daily water needs for your family. If you have not calculated these needs already there is a very simple way

A person should consume 1 gallon of water per day.

With hygiene usage prepare for 2.5 gallons of water per person per day.

REHYDRATION

All of your dehydrated foods will need a period of rehydration to bring them back to life. You will need to boil water and add this water to the ingredients. It's very important to stir your ingredients very thoroughly to allow there is not a clump of dried ingredients in the corner or at the bottom.

Once the ingredients are mixed with the boiling water you will want to cover this as well. The heat and the trapped steam will heat can rehydrate the ingredients.

With a family of four this can add up pretty quickly. You are going to have to look at water procurement as a total process. If you depend on one method for all your water needs, you must work much harder. There are several processes and methods for access to water.

STORING WATER

It takes a tremendous amount of space to gather all the water you will need. Storage should be a part of your water procurement process but unless you have a facility dedicated to water storage I wouldn't even think about it.

They make incredible vessels if you do decide to go this route. There are stackable bricks that can be filled with water. There are also cans and boxes filled with water. Water storage is a big deal in the commercial world. Explore the options out there if you are interested in water storage.

FILTERING WATER

A powerful and portable water filter is crucial to a full functioning water procurement process. This filter will be taken to various water sources near your home. All the water you can travel must be filtered at the source or moved not sanitized and filtered at home. In most cases the water will need to be boiled as well. Another option is to invest in a larger gravity fed filter where water can be hauled to your home and filtered on demand. These filters are also some of the most powerful. The gravity fed filter can hold a tremendous amount of water as well.

WATER CATCHMENT

The best available water resource is that which falls from the sky. Rainwater comes to us purified from the clouds above. It's not until it touches our world that it becomes contaminated. Building a water catchment system is one of the best ways to take advantage of the rainwater. If you are in an area that gets many inches of water per year this system could fill most of your needs.

WATER PURIFICATION

Beyond air, there is no resource more precious than water. Clean water is also crucial to sanitation and hygiene as well. Water used to bath is much different that water used to drink. Most unprocessed sources of water contain parasites and bacteria that can make you very sick. These illnesses have the potential to kill you or those in your party.

The only way to avoid such illness is to filter and purify your water. There are many ways to achieve this and we will discuss several in this portion.

WATER SOURCES

Before begin talking about how to best filter and purify water, you must understand source. Where and how you source, your water can make a massive difference on the finished product. If given the choice between these two water sources which do you think would be the better choice:

Clear mountaintop stream that running through a small stream in high elevation

OR

Stagnate pond with low visibility that is shared by other wild or farm animals

In comparing these two questions you begin to understand the difference in source. You may be surprised to find this out but both sources can kill you if not filtered. Parasites live on mount tops as well as in dirty old ponds. Don't be deceived by clear water.

BIO FILTER

Of the many ways that you can filter water the bio filter comes directly from the world around you. The basic breakdown of a bio filter is the creation of layers that will grab things like sticks, pebbles and smaller sediment in the water. A basic bio filter can be made in a tied off sleeve, sock or other type of container. The layers should go into the container in this order which will allow the finest filtration to happen last.

1. Pulverized charcoal

2. Sand

3. Small pebbles

4. Larger rocks

5. Torn grasses

Water will still need to be boiled after it has been filtered. You can also filter several times to get a cleaner end product.

PORTABLE FILTER

You could also carry a water filter in your pack. There are many great options on the market. Most filters need to be cleaned first before use so be sure you take this step and follow the manufacturer's instructions.

ACTIVATED CHARCOAL

There is more absorbent surface area in activated charcoal than in any other substance used for filtration. Having even a small amount of this in your pack will allow you to get a better filter on any source of water.

BOILING WATER

The final step of water purification is to boil the water to kill all bacteria and parasites. Make sure that your water comes to a rolling boil before taking it off the heat. This is critical to assuring the water will be safe to drink.

Be sure to pour this water into a clean container. Dumping it back into the source container will simply contaminate it again. Remember viruses and bacteria multiply quickly.

IMMEDIATE SOLUTIONS

Being able to purify water does not mean you shouldn't carry your own clean water. There are a few circumstances that can affect your access to water. You could also carry a LifeStraw. These small straws allow you to take an immediate drink without having to boil the water.

Also look into purification tablets. These can be kept in your bag and when dropped into water they kill all of the bacteria and pathogens.

No matter which method you utilize in purifying water be sure that you are proficient. Not having access to water can leave you dehydrated and dead in a matter of days. Drinking dirty water can also be your undoing.

HOMEMADE BERKEY FILTER

Not only should personal water filters be part of your survival plans but you should also have larger water filter systems for your home and group. Berkey makes a tremendous filtration system. The great thing about their system is that you can buy the whole system or you can just buy the filters. Berkey filters and five-gallon buckets should be stored at your bugout location. These two things combined, with a few other elements can create a homemade Berkey filter.

You will need the following items to create your homemade Berkey water filter.

- Two 5-gallon food grade buckets

- Two lids for the buckets

- A pair of Black Berkey filter elements

- A food grade spigot

The first step in turning this collection of materials into a water filter is to drill two ½ inch holes into the bottom of the one bucket and into the top of one of the lids.

Next drill a ¾ inch hole on into the buck that has not been drilled into yet. This will be for your food grade spigot. This is the entirety of the drilling necessary for this project.

Attach the spigot using a food grade sealant. Remember, you are going to be pouring your pristine, filtered water through this spigot.

After that, install the two Berkey filter elements into the bucket with the two holes drilled into it.

At this point you can begin to assemble your filter.

Close the undrilled lid over the bucket with the filters. Sit that bucket on top of your next bucket. The bucket below should have a lid with ½ inch holes that line up with the filter holes. The filter tubes will extend into the second bucket if they are lined up right.

Finally, fill the top bucket with water. It will slowly begin to drip down to the lower buck. After a while you will have a five-gallon bucket of water that has been filtered using your own homemade filter.

HOME MADE BERKEY FILTER

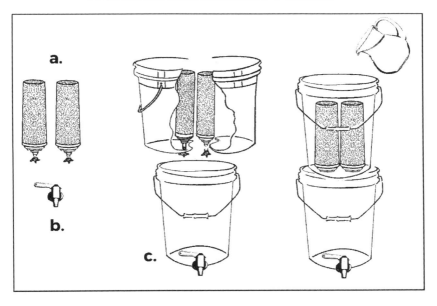

a. **TWO BLACK BERKEY FILTER ELEMENTS**

b. **FOOD GRADE SPIGOT**

c. **FIVE GALLON BUCKET**

LOGISTICS

"Leaders win through logistics. Vision, sure. Strategy, yes. But when you go to war, you need to have both toilet paper and bullets at the right time. In other words, you must win through superior logistics." – Tom Peters

We are not necessarily going to be involved in a physical conflict, none the less, survival situations are a battle. Ensuring that the group has the foodstuff, individual collective equipment to survive is vital to their long-term survival. As such, the group's Quartermaster should be chosen wisely. He should be, or become, experienced at forecasting the group's supplies. Additionally, he should develop a method of tracking these supplies. This system must be transparent and fully available to leadership and other group members for review. In addition to tracking supplies, the quartermaster must have knowledge on storing the items for long term survival. One example is fuel. The Quartermaster must understand the temperature and stabilizers needed for different types of fuel. They must understand the proper storage of food. Though each section is responsible for the stocking of special equipment, the logistics cell must have a working knowledge of these requirements.

An example of this is the Communications Chief is responsible for the radio systems and any spare parts needed. The Communications Chief is also often in charge of stockpiling and managing batteries for the group. Though this is the Communications Chief responsibility, the Quartermaster must understand these requirements and forecasting.

The Quartermaster is often the Camp Mayor. The Camp Mayor ensures the group members have conveniences on camp, serviceable vehicles, and works closely with food services in managing and forecasting food stores.

Larger group's means the group would need a larger logistics cell to help split these duties. A final word on this is to reiterate that the management and use of the group's goods must be transparent to all.

TRACKING GROUP SUPPLIES

Managing and tracking group supplies is vital to long term survival.

INVENTORY

Your groups supplies are working inventory. It's important that someone in your group be responsible for managing that inventory. This inventory manager will be responsible for three main duties. Each will affect the future of your inventory and the group's ability to plan. The three duties are counting, adjusting and forecasting.

If you can manage these three tasks you will be able to completely plan for the days to come. By better understanding your inventory and your group's supplies you can also plan for resource runs or resource purchases based on your par levels.

Par levels are another very important part of managing survival inventory. You establish a par based on how many of one item you need to survive a given time. These par levels will depend on the time frame you measure it by.

EXAMPLE:

My group needs 56 ounces of dry rice per week or 3 ½ pounds. This amount of rice is 2 oz. uncooked per day for 4 people. This means my par level for one week of rice is 3 1/2lbs. If I am below this par level for the week I must get more rice or come up with another options.

Let's talk about our three inventory duties and the best ways to do each. These are vital practices managing your inventory correctly.

COUNTING

The most fundamental part of tracking your supplies is counting them. Without an actual count on supplies adjusting and forecasting become irrelevant. The process of counting must be planned and thorough. If something is missed your count will be botched as well.

Set a time and place for supply counts either each day or each week depending on the size of your group. The smaller the group the less inventory you will have to manage. If you are managing a sizeable group over 5 adults you may consider counting supplies at the end of each day.

Count sheets help but in a survival situation that might not be possible. You will want to keep a pen and pad in your pack and maybe in a zip lock. This will become your inventory documentation.

ADJUSTING

After your count is complete you will want to look at what your previous inventory was from the day or the week before. This will tell you exactly how much of each item was used. Early on this information is crucial as it will tell you your family's actual needs. Until you are in the survival scenario your needs are merely conjecture.

Once you have established your new count and compared it to the old count you can adjust your inventory. If your math is right and everyone is honest things should balance out. In other words, you had 4 datrax bars and your party ate 2 today, you also counted 2 today. That is balanced. If you ate 2 and only one was left over either someone lied or lost a bar. Adjust the standing inventory for what was actually counted.

After adjustments, you want an honest inventory.

FORECASTING

Finally, you will be able to use your inventory to forecast how long you can travel or survive with your supplies. Based on your numbers it will be easy to forecast how long you can go before things like food, water and ammunition run out. By referring to your par levels you should easily be able to figure this out.

SURVIVAL CACHE

Whether you establish a base of operation or have decided to follow a preplanned route, the use of survival caches can make a tremendous difference. In a survival situation, there will not be many places to get resources from. You may find that travel with your pack is a tremendous effort if you are carrying all the ammo, food and supplies you will need to be successful. Your ability to perform and your endurance will have tremendous effect on outcomes.

The survival cache is a container that can be hidden, buried or disguised easily. This container is filled with diverse types of resources that will aid in completing the mission at hand. It will also alleviate the stresses on your person. The survival cache can be filled with critical items that won't add weight to your pack.

This portion will discuss the creation, placement and utilization of these caches. These caches will not only help in you rearm and refuel they will also help with morale. A well placed, full cache can change the mood and feel of a survival operation.

CHOOSING THE RIGHT CACHE

To be sure you are creating the right cache you must first identify your needs. If your cache cannot protect your resources from the elements it will fail and most likely you will fail as well. When producing the cache, ask yourself the following questions:

- Where am I hiding this cache?

- What am I storing inside?

- How long will it be hidden?

- How will I retrieve it?

If you are storing resources that must be kept water tight you will need to consider that in the creation of your cache.

One of the best ways to make a cache is from PVC pipe. These come in diverse sizes and can be cut to meet specific needs. They can hold everything from canned goods to full length rifles. By using a nice water proof sealant and some PVC caps you will be able to keep water out indefinitely.

HIDING THE CACHE

As important as the makeup of the cache so too is the location in which you hide it. If you hide it in a place that is too inconspicuous you may not be able to find it upon your return. Utilize major landmark or sturdy landmarks of great significance to you. Maybe a giant oak or a small cave. Remember, the earth moves and changes a lot. Be sure to store your cache in an area that will keep its shape and form even in the events of a disaster.

- Caches can be buried

- Caches can be paved over

- Caches can be built into structures

- Caches can also be camouflaged and made to look like other things

RESTOCK

Caches must also be restocked. This will not happen at the time of use but I would advise taking the cache with you now and hiding later. If you are being watched or tracked they will see the disturbed location and this will allow them to return to this location to wait for you or your next cache.

No matter how you handle your survival cache protocols be sure to include this powerful resource in your plans. They can extend your mission and give you unparalleled range of operations.

AFTER ACTION REVIEW

It is no accident that at the conclusion to this manual we will discuss the after-action review (AAR). The AAR is a structured discussion of an event to determine what happened and why it happened. The AAR should identify strengths and weaknesses alike. All personnel involved in the event would be present and part of the discussion. Group members are more likely to learn by participating in the discussion as opposed to a one-way evaluation. Often an evaluation only gives one viewpoint and not the best forum for an honest assessment. To begin with, the following questions should be answered.

- What was the plan?

- Timeline of events of what actually happened.

- What caused the differences?

Following these questions should be a period of discussion of what worked, what didn't work and 'why?' The answers to these questions should then in turn lead into changes to the future plan or outline future training needed. Finally, the leader should go around the room and ask one or two individuals for a "sustain" or "improve" for the event. Once the AAR is complete, the leader can give the way forward. This way forward may be as simple as specified tasks that need to be completed or an all-encompassing plan going forward.

This book outlines by chapter the different pieces needed to be prepared. Use this book as a template and develop your individual group's way forward. It is important to establish your physical location for your group ensuring you have a primary and an alternate location. Once your core cadre has been identified, develop your section plan, including the refined SOP of what should be stored and where. Cadre should also develop a training plan that shares their unique knowledge.

Prioritize training by the time available. Weapons handling, IFAK use, and individual security SOP's should be taught first. As a leader, constantly remind your members that **in all that we do, security should come first**. It is very easy to become complacent. Once the individual SOP's have been taught, cadre members should be allotted time to cross train group members. After every training event, an AAR should be conducted. Any needed retraining should then be annotated and conducted as time allows. Once training has been completed, rehearsals should be conducted. It is through these rehearsals and AAR's that we validate the plan.

Like all plans, this book will evolve. There are sections left out I wanted to add and parts I would like to clarify. Like stated in the introduction, the 80% plan actioned is better than the 100% plan that is never completed. I hope this book has been value added and left you with the understanding that it isn't the tactics that are dangerous, it is the organization.

I appreciate your time and trust you have found this book value added. If you did find it helpful, please take a second and give a review. I would also like to hear from you. Check out the website at survivalsop.com or email direct at;

editor@survivalsop.com

Thank you again!

51119904R00146

Made in the USA
Lexington, KY
01 September 2019